UNDERSTANDING ADOLESCENCE

UNDERSTANDING ADOLESCENCE

RONALD L. KOTESKEY

VICTOR BOOKS ®

A DIVISION OF SCRIPTURE PRESS PUBLICATIONS INC.
USA CANADA ENGLAND

Scripture quotations are taken from the *Holy Bible, New International Version,*
© 1973, 1978, 1984, International Bible Society. Used by permission of Zondervan
Bible Publishers.

Recommended Dewey Decimal Classification: 301.4315
Suggested Subject Heading: ADOLESCENCE

Library of Congress Catalog Card Number: 86-63139
ISBN: 0-89693-249-4

CONTENTS

To Keith,
Cheryl,
and Kent,
my own adolescents

PREFACE

As our children began becoming adolescents, I read everything I could about adolescence. As a psychologist I read developmental psychology and was disappointed. Although psychologists described adolescence well, they had few good answers to the problems so many teens and their parents face. I read the Bible, but the Bible said nothing about adolescence.

I finally realized that neither psychology nor Christianity understood adolescence. Only as I studied how adolescence had developed was I able to understand it. I also discovered actions parents could take to help their teenagers. These are not new techniques, but ones that have worked for thousands of years.

I am simply unable to name everyone who has contributed to my thinking regarding this book. Don Joy first triggered it. Students and friends helped immensely as they reacted to ideas I proposed. Asbury College generously provided a work leave during which I wrote the first draft. Students in my classes read the manuscript, pointed out errors, and made suggestions. Of course, I owe the most to my own family. My wife, Bonnie, was my coworker in rearing our own adolescents. Our adolescents Keith, Cheryl, and Kent reacted to the ideas and then lived them out in real life.

CHAPTER ONE

You Don't Understand!

The voices in the hall grew louder and louder as the conversation became more heated. Sitting in the living room, Dad thought, *Oh no. Here we go again!*

Finally, Suzie said, "Mom, you don't understand! You just don't understand! Nobody understands!"

Dad heard the door slam, and he knew that the discussion between parent and teenager was over.

Left standing in the hall, Mom thought, *That's just a cop-out.* But Suzie was right. Mom did not understand. Neither did Dad. Suzie's teachers and minister did not understand either. Of course, Suzie herself did not understand. Hardly anyone in our culture understands adolescence.

If he would pull the dictionary from the bookcase, Dad would read that an adolescent is "a boy or girl from puberty to adulthood." He might think, *There's the problem. Even though she looks like a woman, she's still a girl.*

Would Dad understand then? No! Unfortunately, even the dictionary would add to his confusion. Do *you* understand? Probably not.

This scene could play in any one of thousands of homes,

perhaps in yours. Even if you have checked the dictionary, you probably do not understand. Much has changed during the last century or two. The dictionary tells you the current meaning of *adolescence*, but it does not tell you the rest of the story. Since the definition includes puberty and adulthood, you need to know more about both.

What and When Is Puberty?

Today we think of puberty as the time when people are first able to have children. The dictionary tells us that, but it also tells us that the word *puberty* comes from a Latin word meaning "adult." That is, among the Romans and throughout history, puberty was the beginning of adulthood itself, not the beginning of a stage between childhood and adulthood.

Not only has the meaning of puberty changed, but so has its age. Men may not always realize when they start producing sperm, but women can hardly help noticing their first menstrual period, which is closely related to when they start producing eggs. Although writers have mentioned the beginning of menstruation for more than 2000 years, scientists have studied it carefully only during the last 200 years. They have found that puberty now occurs much earlier than it did a century or two ago.

Before 1850 the average woman first menstruated at about sixteen years of age. Dr. Grace Wyshak and Dr. Rose Frisch at the Harvard Medical School and the Harvard Center for Population Studies reviewed more than 200 studies including more than 200,000 women between 1795 and 1981 ("Evidence for a Secular Trend in Age of Menarche," *The New England Journal of Medicine,* April 29, 1982, pp. 1033-1035). Not a single one of the sixty-five studies done before 1880 found an average age below fourteen and a half. Many were seventeen or more. By 1950 however, the average was down to about twelve and a half or thirteen.

Puberty in men is not as obvious and has not been studied as much. However, when Bach was choirmaster at St. Thomas Church in Leipzig more than 200 years ago, boys often sang soprano until they were seventeen. Tenors and basses were men whose voices had already changed. Altos were those whose voices were changing. In 1744, Bach had ten altos, the youngest was fifteen and the oldest nineteen. Men's voices changed at about seventeen years of age then, but at about thirteen or fourteen now (J.M. Tanner, *A History of the Study of Human Growth,* Cambridge University Press). This change takes place at about the age of puberty.

All of this means that people today experience puberty about three or four years earlier than they did only a century or two ago. Figure 1 shows how this change has taken place. The decrease in age during the last two hundred years is a summary of more than two hundred studies. The stable age before that is an estimate.

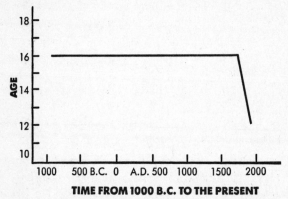

Figure 1. Major changes in average age of puberty in women during the last 3000 years. Puberty in men would be about two years later.

What and When Is Adulthood?

Just as the dictionary gave us a surprise about puberty, so it does about adulthood. Although the words *adolescent* and *adult* appear to be very different, they come from the *same* Latin word, one meaning "to grow." *Adolescent* originally meant "growing one," referring to the sudden growth spurt at about the age of puberty. *Adult* meant "grown one," a person past his or her growth spurt.

As we read the current meanings of the word *adult*, we find two. First, it means a person grown to full size. Second, it means a person who has come of age. The problem is that our society has separated these two meanings. This separation of the two meanings is what we now mean by adolescence, the period between the time children become adults and the time we treat them as adults.

Although treating someone as an adult has many aspects, in this chapter let us concentrate on one we can trace throughout history. Since adolescence begins with puberty, a sexual event, let us look at when we allow people to marry, another sexual event—one tied closely to being an adult. As we look at the minimum legal age of marriage during 3000 years of history, we will see how we have invented adolescence only during the last century.

The *Talmud*, the vast collection of the oral law of the Jews, tells us that the ancient Hebrews could marry at puberty. Not only were they allowed to marry then, but they were encouraged to do so. God told Moses to tell the Israelites, "Do not degrade your daughter by making her a prostitute" (Lev. 19:29). Rabbi Akiba interpreted this as a warning against a delay in marrying a daughter who has reached puberty. He reasoned that since she was sexually mature, she might become unchaste if she remained unmarried (Sanhedrin 76a).

The rabbis taught that one should first study Torah (the first five books of the Bible) and then marry. The ideal was to study Torah at fifteen and marry at eighteen. Of course, we must remember that puberty for men was probably at seventeen or eighteen then. However, those rabbis said that if a man could not live without a wife, "he should first marry and then study" (Aboth V, Kiddushin 29b).

Not only would premarital sex become a problem if people did not marry at puberty, but so would sexual fantasy. Rabbi Huna said that anyone not married by age twenty would spend all his days in sinful thoughts (Kiddushin 29b). Rabbi Hisda claimed to be superior to other rabbis because he had married at sixteen. He said he would have been even better if he had married at fourteen, because he would have been free of impure thoughts (Kiddushin 29b-30a).

Two thousand years ago under Roman law, women could marry at twelve and men at fourteen. A thousand years ago under English law it was the same. Two hundred years ago under common law in the United States it was still the same—women could marry at twelve and men at fourteen. For 3000 years, the minimum legal age for marriage did not change. Of course, not everyone married at twelve or fourteen, just as everyone does not marry at eighteen today.

Then just as the age of puberty was decreasing, laws *increasing* the minimum legal age for marriage were passed in the United States and Europe. This was a part of the creation of adolescence. ✳ Although they were adults and had been treated as adults for thousands of years, teenagers were redefined as "children."

By the middle of the twentieth century the most common minimum legal ages for marriage were eighteen for women and twenty-one for men. This difference in age for women and men, like that of earlier laws, showed an awareness that women matured earlier than men. However, in the 1960s in nearly every state the ages were changed to eighteen for both men and women.

Figure 2 adds the minimum legal age for marriage to the curve for average age of puberty. Notice that at the same time that the age of puberty was decreasing, the minimum legal age for marriage was increasing. *This* was the creation of adolescence. For the first ✳ time people were not allowed to make adult decisions at the age of puberty.

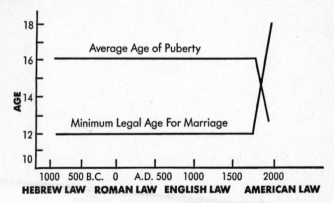

Figure 2. Major changes in average age of puberty and minimum legal age for marriage for women during the last 3000 years. The ages for men would be about two years later (except in the case of marriage during the last 20 years).

15

Notice that we did not just coin a new word to describe something that had always existed. We did just the opposite. We took an old word and used it to mean something that we had just created. *Adolescence* now refers to the teen years, during which we treat people as children even though they are adults. It is not a matter of what we call teenagers; it is how we treat them.

Historian John Demos of Brandeis University and Virginia Demos in the Program of Human Development at Harvard University put it this way. "The concept of adolescence, as generally understood and applied, did not exist before the last two decades of the nineteenth century. One could almost call it an invention of that period" ("Adolescence in Historical Perspective," *Journal of Marriage and the Family*, 1969, *31*, pp. 632–638).

In the journal of the American Academy of Arts and Sciences, David Bakan said, "The idea of adolescence as an intermediary period of life starting at puberty . . . is the product of modern times. . . . [It developed] in the latter half of the nineteenth and the early twentieth century . . . to prolong the years of childhood" ("Adolescence in America: From Idea to Social Fact," *Daedalus*, 1971, *100*, pp. 979–995).

Adolescence has been created and handed to us. Like Shelley's Dr. Frankenstein, our culture has created a monster and is having trouble controlling it. Some people call adolescence "a period of temporary insanity between childhood and adulthood." They are right, but it is not the teenager that is insane. It is our culture. Our crazy culture invented adolescence about a century ago, and now we do not know what to do with it.

An Interlude—or Storm and Stress?

Let us consider another situation that happens in many homes. Early one warm spring evening Al, a high school freshman, and his father are talking.

"I'll be glad when I'm out of school and can get a job. I'm tired of being a kid," said Al.

"You don't know how good you have it!" said Dad. "I have to work to support myself, your mother, and all you kids. All you have to do is eat, sleep, and have fun."

"It's no fun!" said Al. "I'm a man, but everyone treats me like a boy. I want to work, but I have to go to school."

"If you want to work," said Dad, "mow the lawn. Then after you study your algebra, you can hoe the garden. That's work."

"That's not what I mean. I want to make money, and to make a difference in the world, " said Al. "I want to do something, but no one will let me."

Who is right, Al or his father? People cannot agree. Some say one, and some the other.

Some people see adolescence as a time-out between childhood and adulthood. Not burdened with responsibility, teenagers can take time to think seriously about life. They can carefully consider careers and choose the one best for them. They have time to learn through the free education open to them. They can date many different people to choose their husbands and wives. In short, it is a wonderful interlude before the realities of life hit home.   ✳

Many adults, caught up in their world of work and responsibility, think teenagers have it made. How nice not to have to go to work every morning! How nice not to have to feed a growing adolescent! They say that teenagers do not realize how good they have it.

Psychoanalyst Erik Erikson called adolescence a "psychosocial moratorium." He said it was a_delay of adult commitments, a time in which people could try different roles to discover where they belonged in society. It was characterized by "selective permissiveness" by society and by "provocative playfulness" by youth. ✳ Adolescents could act irresponsibly in some ways, and adults would not be very upset about it. It was a time of sports, of horseplay, of cliques, and of parties.

However, not everyone has such a positive view of adolescence. Psychologist G. Stanley Hall wrote the first major work on adolescence in 1904. He characterized adolescence as being a period of *Sturm und Drang,* "storm and stress." Rather than being an idyllic ✳ calm between childhood and adulthood, it was in his view a stormy time.

The National Commission on Youth, established by the Kettering Foundation, said that becoming an adult is difficult even in the best of times. Unfortunately, it is the worst of times for many

17

modern youth. For many teenagers adolescence is characterized by confusion, pain, and uncertainty. It is a time when social and environmental stress produce great tensions.

Psychologist Arthur Jersild of Columbia University asked adults if they would do differently if they could relive their adolescence, given the increased knowledge they now had. All said yes. Then he asked them if they would actually like to relive their adolescence. All said no!

Why would they not like to actually relive it? Because even though they believe they would be able to have a better adolescence, they do not want to go back to being treated like children. Adults do not want to be treated like children, and that is the basic problem of adolescence. ✳

What Does the Bible Say?
As Christians, our first response should be to turn to Scripture. The problem with that is that the Bible does not say anything specific about adolescence. Just as it does not tell us about automobile repair because automobiles did not exist then, it does not tell us about solving the problems of adolescence because, as we have seen, adolescence did not exist then. Unfortunately we sometimes misinterpret Scripture, thinking it is talking about adolescents. Let us consider some Scriptures that seem to be about adolescents but are not, as well as some that would probably mention adolescence if it existed.

In the Old Testament, King Solomon gave much good advice to his son in the early chapters of the Book of Proverbs. He said, "Listen, my son, to your father's instruction and do not forsake your mother's teaching" (Prov. 1:8). "Wisdom is supreme; therefore get wisdom. Though it cost all you have, get understanding" (Prov. 4:7). "Keep to a path far from her [an adultress], do not go near the door of her house" (Prov. 5:8).

Although we might think he was talking to an adolescent, he was not. "May your fountain be blessed, and may you rejoice in the wife of your youth" (Prov. 5:18). "It will save you also from the adultress, from the wayward wife with her seductive words, who has left the partner of her youth and ignored the covenant she made before God" (Prov. 2:16-17). The son was not an unmarried teenager, but a married man, told to rejoice in the "wife of his youth." The adultress was a woman who had left the "partner of her youth."

There are several passages in the Bible where we might expect to find a reference to the period of time between childhood and adulthood, but such a reference never appears. For instance, Moses is never referred to as an adolescent. "When the child grew older, she took him to Pharaoh's daughter and he became her son. She named him Moses, saying, 'I drew him out of the water.' One day, after Moses had grown up, he went out to where his own people were and watched them at their hard labor. He saw an Egyptian beating a Hebrew, one of his own people" (Ex. 2:10-11). In verse ten he was a "child," and by verse eleven he "had grown up." Adolescence simply did not exist in Old Testament times.

Moses' growth is described the same way in the New Testament. "By faith Moses' parents hid him for three months after he was born, because they saw he was no ordinary child, and they were not afraid of the king's edict. By faith Moses, when he had grown up, refused to be known as the son of Pharaoh's daughter" (Heb. 11:23-24). In verse twenty-three he was a "child," and by verse twenty-four he "had grown up."

When the Apostle John was looking for a way of talking about people at different stages of maturity, he talked about children, young men, and fathers (1 John 2:12-14). We might think of the "young men" as adolescents, but they really were *men*. They were people in the prime of life. Like Solomon, John was not talking about people between puberty and adulthood, but about adults.

The Apostle Paul told us about his development. "When I was a child, I talked like a child, I thought like a child, I reasoned like a child. When I became a man, I put childish ways behind me" (1 Cor. 13:11). Why did he not tell us what he was like as an adolescent? Because he never was an adolescent!

Of course, these passages of Scripture do not prove that adolescence did not exist, but they illustrate what we found earlier in the chapter. Before the nineteenth century we had childhood and adulthood, but no adolescence. We might picture the situation in their day as in the first part of Figure 3. Moses, Solomon, John, Paul, and others at that time went directly from childhood to adulthood. They were teenagers, but they were never adolescents. When they were in their teens, they were adults.

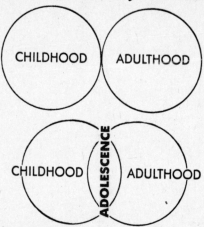

Figure 3. Childhood, adolescence, and adulthood before (top) and after (bottom) the creation of adolescence.

As you see in the second part of figure 3, today we have a period during which childhood and adulthood overlap. This invention of adolescence has created problems primarily in the areas of identity, sexuality, work, and school. As long as we have adolescence, we will face these problems. Since our culture created adolescence, it can do away with it in the future, but that will not help those of us who are facing life with our adolescents today.

Although the Bible does not talk about adolescence as a stage of life, it certainly talks about teenagers. Of course, it treats them like adults, not like children. It is relevant to their lives, but has nothing to say to our practice of treating them like children. It treats them as responsible adults, and we should too.

What Can Parents Do?

The basic thing you can do to help your adolescents now is to treat them as much like adults as possible. Obviously there are some restrictions on what the law and other people will let you do. For example, the law will not allow them to work for wages, but you can see that they learn to work at home. Although they cannot legally earn much money, you can still see that they learn how to handle money wisely. The law will not allow them to marry, but you can help them learn how to get along in a family relationship. Even if other people expect your teenagers to act irresponsibly, you can expect them to be responsible.

Your first reaction may be, "This will never work. Expecting teenagers to act like adults is expecting too much!" I disagree. It worked for thousands of years, so why would it not work today? Treating teenagers like children in our modern culture clearly is not working. Why not try something that has been proven to work for thousands of years in many different cultures? Most of us keep using something that does not work (treating teenagers like children) because we do not like being different from those around us. We are more comfortable with something familiar, even if it does not work.

You may say, "Our culture today is much more complex than it was in former times. Teenagers simply cannot act like adults now as they did then!" Again, I disagree. Life has always been complex. We only try to flatter ourselves by thinking that it is worse now than then. Could we organize a society to rule most of the world as the Romans did? Throughout history teenagers have been able to live as adults in many different cultures. The world is not so different that they cannot do so now.

Expect the best. Your expectations as a parent are probably the most important factors in your teenagers acting like adults. In the next chapter, we will see that people usually behave as others expect them to. However, even if teenagers behave like adults, you will probably see them as acting like children—if you think of them as children. This was dramatically demonstrated in a study done by psychologist David Rosenhan ("On Being Sane in Insane Places," *Science,* 1973, *179,* pp. 250-258).

Dr. Rosenhan invented a "mental illness" and had mentally healthy people admit themselves to a dozen mental hospitals by pretending to be crazy in the first interview. After that, they all acted perfectly normal while they were in the mental hospitals. They were kept in the hospitals for anywhere from a week to nearly two months and given a total of 2100 pills. Although other patients recognized that they were normal and accused them of being reporters, none of the doctors or nurses did. Patients in mental hospitals are supposed to be crazy. Even if they act normal, doctors and nurses see them as acting crazy. In the same way, when you expect your teens to be immature and irresponsible, even when they act responsibly, you will not see it.

Just as you can make people worse (crazy or immature) by expecting little of them, you can make them better by expecting more. Psychologist Robert Rosenthal has investigated this in many experiments (Robert Rosenthal and Lenore Jacobson, *Pygmalion in the Classroom,* Holt, Rinehart and Winston). In one of his early experiments he gave students in several schools an IQ test, then *randomly* picked out about 20% of the students. He told the teachers the test showed these students to be late bloomers and that they would suddenly get smarter that year. (He lied—the test showed no such thing.)

The teachers later rated these students as having a better chance of becoming successful, more curious, more interesting, and happier than the other students in the class. They also tended to see these students as better adjusted and more appealing. It is no surprise to learn that their grades went up. But when Dr. Rosenthal tested them eight months later, their IQs went up too. Just expecting them to be more intelligent actually raised their IQ scores.

In other experiments even rats learned faster if their trainers believed they were smart than if their trainers thought they were dumb. If you believe your teenagers are adults and expect them to act like it, they can—and will. Expect responsible, adult behavior, and you will get it. Expect irresponsible, childish behavior, and you will get it.

Do things with them. You probably say, "I already do things with them." But do you do things with them, or do they do things with you? Remember that your teenagers are people too. They would rather do some things than others. The crucial thing is that it be the adolescent who decides what you do. Let us consider some examples.

My oldest son, Keith, became interested in photography. I had always been a "point-and-shoot" photographer, and I sent my film off for developing and printing. Keith wanted a single lens reflex camera so he could control the f-stop and the exposure time. He wanted to develop and print his own pictures. We did it. Some of our early attempts were hilarious, but I learned along with him and discovered the whole fascinating world of developing and printing pictures.

A neighboring family was at a park where Diana Ross and the Supremes were singing. They had spent the whole day at various attractions, including attending a concert by the Supremes. As they were about to leave, Joan, their teenage daughter, wanted to hear the concert again. The tired Mom and Dad wanted to flop down on a bed, not sit through a concert they had already heard once that day, but they went again. They did something with Joan, and it was a turning point in their relationship.

Contrast this with Don, another friend of mine. Don's father took him fishing every weekend. This sounds like a teenager's dream—but Don hated fishing. He wanted to stay home, but every Saturday they were out trolling. If you had asked, his father would have told you he spent every weekend with Don. He did not. Don spent every weekend with him. The most important thing is who has decided what you do.

Share your understanding. Let us now return to our opening story. Suzie was right. Nobody understood. After reading this far, you should have an understanding of the problem, even though it may not yet be clear what you can do to solve it. The problem is adolescence itself. The scene we saw at the beginning of the chapter, so common now, would have been rare more than a hundred years ago. Most people then went directly from childhood to adulthood, so disagreements between parents and adolescents did not happen. There were no adolescents.

Who was right when Al and his father were discussing the nature of adolescence? Is adolescence an interlude, or is it a time of storm and stress? Both were right. It is an interlude between childhood and full adulthood, but too often it is a stressful interlude. It is an interlude that looks good when one is not in it, but feels bad when one is living through it.

Now that you have an understanding of the problem, you need to begin to share that insight with your own adolescents, so they will develop some self-understanding. Show them how the ages of puberty and adulthood have changed, and how they are caught in the middle. Tell them that you want to work with them to help them through this time that society has forced on all of you.

If you have children, begin to share with them as well. Preparing them for what is ahead will make adolescence easier when it comes in their lives. As they become adolescents, you can get a head start on solving the problems that are likely to arise.

Expecting the best from your teenagers, doing things with them, and sharing your understanding with them will not automatically make adolescence painless. Our culture has given us a very difficult task as parents. The suggestions in this book will make the task easier, not easy.

CHAPTER TWO
Adolescents Are Adults

Mark was president of the youth group at church and had a meeting there in less than an hour. He was still not home from track team practice. He had agreed to tell the coach that he had to leave early so he could be on time to lead the youth group.

Mom and Dad realized that it would be hard for a high school junior to tell his coach that he had to leave practice early. As the minutes ticked away, Mom and Dad became more concerned that Mark be at church for the youth meeting. Finally Dad said, "I'm going to drive over to the school and talk to the coach myself."

As Dad drove up to the school, Mark was just coming out. Seeing his father, Mark indignantly said, "What are you doing here? I'm an adult! I can take care of myself!"

"I thought it would be easier for a father to talk to the coach. It's hard for a team member to tell a coach what to do," Dad tried to explain.

"You still think of me as a little kid," said Mark, not quite forgiving his father for not having confidence in him.

Mark's dad was not alone in thinking of his teenager as a child. Nearly everywhere we turn we see something telling us that teens are children. A cover story of *Time* magazine (December 9, 1985) was "Children Having Children," subtitled "Teen Pregnancy in America." I have seen television broadcasts with the same title on both the local and the national news. The fact is that children cannot have children. Only adults, people who have passed puberty, can have babies.

David Gergen, Managing Editor for News, wrote the editorial, "Childhood Lost" for *U.S. News & World Report* (October 28, 1985, p. 78). He used the words "child" and "children" eight times in his editorial. In the article he talked about "teenage pregnancies," "youngsters between 15 and 19," "America's 17-year-olds," "high-school-dropout rates," "teenage girls," and people at "their 18th birthday." Clearly teenagers were children for him.

Leaving K-Mart I picked up a pamphlet put out by the "Lost Child Network." In large black letters it said, "Please call us if you think you've seen one of our children." Four "children" were pictured, and their ages were five, seven, twenty-two, and twenty-eight. The two older ones had been missing since they were seventeen. Are they children in their twenties, or even when they were seventeen?

As parents, we may look at our adolescents and ask ourselves, "Are they really adults? If they are, why don't they act like it?" Even though people treated teenagers like adults for thousands of years, teens today just do not act like adults. Maybe teenagers are just maturing earlier sexually, but in other ways they are even less mature than they used to be.

Are They Adults Physically?

In the last chapter we saw that people reach puberty several years earlier than they did a century ago. Perhaps that earlier maturity is only sexual, and other physical developments occur no earlier. That is not the case. Sexual development at puberty, accompanied by the growth spurt, is one of the last physical developments.

You need go no further than your medicine cabinet to see that the pharmaceutical world considers your adolescent an adult. Bayer aspirin has a "children's dosage" and an "adult dose." Ages are not given for the adult dose, but the oldest one for children is

"11 to 12 years 1½ tablets." Adults can take 2 tablets, so apparently anyone over 12 years old is an adult. Tylenol has an adult dose of up to 2 tablets and "children (6-12) ½ to 1 tablet." Again people over 12 are adults.

The dosages on decongestants show the problem drug companies have in treating teenagers as adults. Sudafed has a children's dosage and another one for "adults and children 12 years of age ✳ and over." Robitussin has the same thing. It has a dosage for "children 6 to under 12 years" and one for "adults and children 12 years of age and over." The phrase "children 12 years of age and over" shows that they see teenagers as adults physically, but do not consider them adults socially.

Restaurant owners realize that children become adults at about ✳ the age of twelve. They know that treating adolescents as children would wipe out their profits. Nearly all restaurants charge teenagers adult prices because managers know that teens eat as much as—or more than—other adults. Any mother can tell you that.

Of course, people continue to change physically after puberty. They continue to grow slightly taller even up to about twenty years of age. You are probably well aware that people continue to put on weight through middle age and even into old age. That does not mean that they are not adults until they stop growing. They are physically adults as teenagers, soon after their growth spurts.

Can They Think Like Adults?

Swiss psychologist Jean Piaget led the study of the development of thinking. He found that the final change in thinking begins at about ✳ the age of puberty (*The Growth of Logical Thinking from Childhood to Adolescence,* Barbel Inhelder and Jean Piaget, Basic Books). Although not everyone reaches this stage of "formal operations" in which they can think abstractly, those who do enter it begin to do so at the age of eleven or twelve.

Of course, Piaget was not the first one to notice that children and adults think differently. Remember how the Apostle Paul described differences between his childhood and adulthood. "When I was a child, I talked like a child, I thought like a child, I reasoned like a child. When I became a man, I put childish ways behind me"

✳

(1 Cor. 13:11). Notice that the major differences he mentioned were in language, thinking, and reasoning. In these he went from being a child to being an adult.

School authorities realize this. They do not allow students to take courses requiring abstract thinking, such as courses in algebra and chemistry, until after the average age of puberty. Trying to take these courses too soon can bring disaster. One college student told me, "I took algebra in eighth grade and had no idea what was going on, so I failed it. I repeated it in ninth and it was simple. I got an A." What had happened was that he matured into the stage of formal operations that year.

Not everyone agrees with Piaget's stages of mental development, but most agree that few, if any, new abilities appear after adolescence. To meaningfully measure the intelligence of adults, psychologists had to use a whole different approach than they used to measure the intelligence of children. The first successful intelligence tests, shortly after 1900 measured a child's "mental age" and divided it by his age in years, giving an intelligence quotient, or IQ.

When the early testers measured the IQs of army recruits in World War I, they were shocked. They found an average mental age of only about fourteen or fifteen among the eighteen-year-old recruits. The testers thought the recruits were mentally retarded. Of course, the problem was that little mental growth takes place beyond puberty. Adolescents are adults, not children, in their thinking.

Can They Make Adult Decisions?

Although teenagers were considered able to make important decisions for thousands of years, today we assume they cannot. In 1979 Chief Justice Warren Burger said that adolescents were not able to "make sound judgments concerning many decisions." He thought of adolescents as being little different from children in their ability to make such decisions.

In spite of this legal opinion, many psychologists have shown that adolescents can make adult decisions. Harvard psychologist Lawrence Kohlberg has studied moral development and proposed several levels of it. The highest level of moral development begins to appear only in adolescence. It is not found in ten-year-olds, but begins to appear by the age of thirteen (*The Philosophy of Moral Development: Moral Stages and the Idea of Justice,* Harper & Row).

People at this level of development can make decisions on the basis of moral principles rather than on the authority of other people. Luther was a defensive lineman on his high school football team. When the coach told the defensive team to take the opposing quarterback out—out of the game, not just out of the play—Luther could not follow that order. He could tackle the quarterback, but he would not bring himself to hurt him enough to get him out of the game. Adolescents can make these kinds of moral decisions. Rather than simply obeying people or rules, they can think about other people's rights and general principles.

Of course, like other adults, adolescents do not make all their moral judgments on the basis of ethical and moral principles. However, adolescents who have matured in their thinking *can* make moral judgments this way. Even people who disagree with the idea of stages of development would agree that the moral judgments of sixteen-year-olds are very similar to those of older adults, and quite different from those of six-year-olds.

Why Don't They Act Like Adults?

At this point you are probably thinking, *If they can think like adults and make moral decisions like adults, why do they act like children? Why don't they act like adults?* The idea that adolescents should act like children is a part of our invention of adolescence. This began about 150 years ago when educators concluded that it was harmful to mature too early and talked about the "disease of precocity."

For nearly a hundred years, people believed that if children developed too rapidly they were ill. If children began to act like adults too soon, they could even go insane. Rather than thinking of such children as "gifted," parents took them out of school and encouraged them to play and do manual labor. They did not want their children to develop the terrible disease of precocity. They did not want "early ripe, early rot."

Between 1900 and 1920 we even started many organizations to turn adolescents from adults into children. Boy Scouts, Girl Scouts, Boys' Clubs, Camp Fire Girls, and boys' and girls' agricultural clubs are only a few of these organizations. With the invention of these, we officially started calling people in their teens "boys" and "girls." In our thinking we changed them from adults into children.

Today we just accept the "fact" that adolescents are to act like children rather than like adults and it becomes a self-fulfilling prophecy. We do not want them to grow up too fast, so they do not. Some people try to slow adolescent development. For example Larry Richards wrote

> Unfortunately, our culture forces teenagers' development too rapidly, especially boy-girl relationships. With my own teens I felt that slowing down adolescence was a positive thing and so I very consciously insulated my teens from the fast pace of growth that adolescent culture assumes.
>
> One way I did this was by not letting them get their driver's licenses until they were out of high school ("The Stages of Adolescence," in *Parents & Teenagers,* Edited by Jay Kesler, Victor Books, p. 157).

We saw the effect of what people expect illustrated dramatically in our community. When our former youth minister's house was "toilet papered," he got angry, chastised the youth group as a whole, found out who did it, and made them clean it up. Not another house was toilet papered for three years. When our new youth minister came, he was surprised that the teens were not toilet papering houses. He challenged them to do his house without getting caught. Within a few months, someone's house was being toilet papered nearly every weekend.

If you expect your teenagers to act like irresponsible children, they will. On the other hand, if you expect them to act like responsible adults, as people did for thousands of years, they will.

Why Are We Always Fighting?

You may have found yourself in repeated conflict with your adolescents and wondered what is wrong with you. Adolescence itself really does involve conflict. The problem is that you probably do not understand the nature of the conflict. You may think that the problem is between you and your teenagers, but your family is only part of a larger problem.

The real conflict is between society and its adolescents. Adolescents are adults, but society treats them like children. Our society has created adolescents but made little provision for them. It has not given them a real role to play. Adolescents are nearly at their peak but not allowed to participate. They are at the starting gate of life with no place to go. Since the gate will be closed for six to ten years, the results of such frustration are predictable.

Such teenagers often become alienated and disliked. Other adults, feeling ill at ease around teenagers, often do not even like to meet a group of teens on the street. They may cross to the other side rather than pass a group of rowdy teens. Parents also feel frustrated because teenagers take time and money, keeping parents from reaching their own goals. Even being a parent of adolescents seems to strike fear into many hearts. A recent book, *How to Live with Your Teenagers,* is subtitled "A Survivor's Handbook for Parents."

Parents have the unenviable position of being frontline troops in this conflict between adolescents and their culture. They are responsible for supporting their teenagers, keeping them quiet, and keeping them in the school system until the adult world has a place for them. The conflict is between adolescents and society, but parents are the focal point. Each adolescent and his or her parents are the available representatives of a larger war.

In the mid 1970s columnist Ann Landers asked her readers, "If you had it to do over again, would you have children?" She was not prepared for more than 10,000 letters, the largest response she had ever received to a question at that time. And 70% said no! The most bitter letters were from parents of adolescents. Formal research has shown similar results about parents being dissatisfied.

Boyd Rollins and Harold Feldman ("Marital Satisfaction Over

the Family Life Cycle," *Journal of Marriage and the Family,* 1970, *32,* pp. 20-28), both professors in human development and family relationships, studied the satisfaction of nearly 800 couples during eight stages of their family life. The first stage was the beginning family, couples married five years or less without children. The last stage was aging families, couples from retirement to the death of the first spouse. They asked people if their present stage in life was "very satisfying."

Satisfaction was high in the early years of marriage until the oldest child was two. Nearly 70% of both husbands and wives reported they were very satisfied then. After that the decline started. The two lowest times were stages five and six. Stage five was "families with teenagers," families in which the oldest child was between thirteen and twenty-one. Stage six was "families as launching centers," the time between when the first child goes until the last one has left home. By stage six, only about 10% reported that they were "very satisfied."

Satisfaction did not begin to increase until the last adolescent was gone, and did not reach the levels of the first years of marriage until retirement. Husbands and wives were least satisfied during their offspring's adolescence. Rollins and Feldman concluded that this was probably more an indication of "satisfaction with parenthood" than of satisfaction with marriage.

Sociologist Karen Renne ("Correlates of Dissatisfaction in Marriage," *Journal of Marriage and the Family,* 1970, *32,* pp. 54-67) studied factors that produced dissatisfaction in marriage in more than 5000 married adults. She found the greatest dissatisfaction in homes with "children under 19 present." The least dissatisfaction was in homes that "had children, but none present now." That is, parents are happiest after their children leave home, and unhappiest when they are adolescents. At that time the parents are on the front lines of the conflict between adolescents and their culture.

What Can Parents Do?

The basic thing you can do is treat your adolescents like adults. Call them "men" and "women" not "kids." Let them make decisions as long as they act like responsible adults. Learning to make decisions, like learning to drive, takes practice. Your teenagers cannot learn to make decisions by just watching you make them. Of course, you have to be sure that you act responsibly yourself to serve as a good model for them.

As a young man, Timothy was a pastor. Paul told him, "Don't let anyone look down on you because you are young, but set an example for the believers in speech, in life, in love, in faith and in purity" (1 Tim. 4:12). Do you look down on your teenagers because they are young? According to the Apostle Paul, you should not.

As a young man, John Mark had started on a missionary trip with Paul and Barnabas. However, he quit and returned to Jerusalem when they got to Perga in Pamphylia. Paul would not accept such irresponsible behavior even from a young person. Later when Paul wanted to go again, "Barnabas wanted to take John, also called Mark, with them, but Paul did not think it was wise to take him, because he had deserted them in Pamphylia and had not continued with them in the work" (Acts 15:37-38).

Some parents let their adolescents make minor decisions, but not ones that will really affect their lives. For example, they let them decide what to wear, or whether to sing in the choir or not. But, when it comes to what courses to take in school, the parents say that the teens cannot make that decision because it really affects the future. We have looked at how teens are mature physically, mentally, and morally, so let us consider the kinds of decisions they can make.

Let them make physical decisions. In terms of physical decisions, allow teens to make decisions about eating and sleeping. As long as they eat nourishing foods, let them choose their own diet. Our own teens cook Sunday dinner on alternate Sundays. They are responsible for everything from planning the menu to cooking the food. If they forget, we all have sandwiches.

It seemed like Gus was always going through the hamburger line for lunch at school instead of going through the regular hot lunch line. Finally, Mom said, "Gus, you need to be more careful to get a balanced diet."

Gus said, "Mom, a cheeseburger with everything has all four

basic food groups." He was right.

You may be able to get teenagers into bed, but you cannot make them sleep. Rather than getting them into bed early—and angry—we have found it better to let them decide how much sleep to get. Of course, that is true only as long as they get enough to not sleep through school and not be hard to live with. People need different amounts of sleep, and about half need less than the traditional eight hours. One of our teens sleeps about six and a half hours a night, another about nine, and both of those are responsible decisions.

When I was a teenager, the light had to be turned out long before I was ready to go to sleep. Although the ceiling light was out, I had a book and a flashlight under the covers. I do not know how many batteries I drained while reading through those evenings.

Encourage them to make "mental decisions." Have teenagers make decisions about what they study. Many teens take piano lessons because their parents wish they (the parents) could play. Lois decided she wanted to play the piano. Her parents agreed to pay for lessons as long as she took them for a full year and practiced regularly without complaining. At the end of the year Lois decided she did not want to play the piano after all, and she wanted to quit. Although her parents thought she would be sorry later, they went along with her decision. Adolescents are adults and must learn to live with the consequences of their decisions.

Have teenagers choose their courses in high school as well as college. Point out the advantages and disadvantages of different courses and majors in light of what they want to do, then let them decide. If they make the wrong choice, they live with it and should not blame you. In the high school office a teacher gave us a stunned look of disbelief when she saw us allow our son to choose an elective speech course over an honors English course. As far as we were concerned, the choice was his, and he could always take an English course in the future.

Include adolescents as full adults in conversations when you have guests. Ask their opinions, and respect what they tell you. Adolescents are to be heard as well as seen. We include them in family decisions about vacations and where to eat out. This helps them to learn to make decisions within the limits of a budget.

Adolescents should be expected to take responsibility for many activities in their lives. They can call and make appointments for the doctor and dentist. Everything from decor to cleanliness of their rooms should be up to them, as long as they take it seriously. Of course, if you expect them to clean it thoroughly once a week and keep it generally picked up the rest of the time, you should do the same with the rest of the house.

You should have a will naming guardians for your teens, and the teens should have a voice in the choice. The guardians we had named for our children lived in a different state by the time they became teenagers. We then asked our teens who they would like as guardians, and all three immediately named different families. After nearly two weeks of discussion, they finally settled on one family. When we asked that family, they (including their teens) discussed it and agreed. Since they may have to live with the guardians, teenagers should have a voice in choosing them.

Help them with moral decisions. Your adolescents must learn to make moral decisions as well. Chances to make these are found nearly every time you turn on the radio or television. We and our teens listen to the words of the singer on the radio. Whether to keep listening or not is a moral decision. We ask, "What values is this television show promoting? Are these ones that we, as Christians, can approve?" If not, we make a moral decision to turn it off or change the channel. If you want to go even further, you can write the sponsor and express your distaste.

When your teens choose their friends and leisure activities, they are making moral decisions. When they choose a movie or a party game, they are making moral decisions, and you need to help them see the implications of their decisions. Even how teens drive is a moral decision. If they drive recklessly, they are a danger not only to themselves, but also to others. If our teens drive safely, we encourage it; but reckless driving means loss of the use of the car.

Encourage your teens to see the moral decisions they make (or will soon be making) politically. Some of those are presented as moral decisions, such as laws on abortion or capital punishment. We have some interesting and heated discussions around the table on these issues, and our positions sometimes conflict. In addition, teens need to see that decisions to build a nuclear weapon or even take the curve out of a county road are moral decisions. The money then cannot be used to help others get food or medical care and may result in the destruction of human life.

Adolescents have the ability to make adult decisions. It is the parent's responsibility to see that the teenagers have all the information they need, and then let the teen make the decision. The only way to learn how to make decisions is to actually make them, and live with the consequences. We must let our teens make important decisions. They are adults and should be treated like adults.

Minimize the Conflict

You essentially have no choice about your assignment to the conflict between adolescents and their culture. Although there will always be some conflict, you can take steps to make it less severe.

One thing you can do is make it clear to your adolescents exactly what the conflict is. Help them to see that the conflict is not just between you and them, but between their culture and adolescents in general. Make it clear that even though society may see them as children, you see them as adults. Treat them as adults, and expect adult behavior from them.

Tell them that you do not like your situation any better than they like theirs. As one psychologist put it, "Misery loves miserable company." If they see that you are acting the way you are only because society demands that of you, they will better understand you, just as you better understand them. Neither of you asked to be placed on the front lines of this cultural conflict.

To carry the war analogy a little further, you may have to lose a few battles to win the war. When you have disagreements with your adolescents, they need to win some. Of course, legally you have the power to tell them what to do, but it is better not to use that power too much. If you do, when they turn eighteen and you do not have that power, they may turn against all that you stand for.

Some battles are not worth winning. Remember the parents of

the 1960s who won the battle of the haircut, but lost their sons. One woman (wearing earrings in her pierced ears) in my class said, "When I was in high school, I wanted my ears pierced, but my father wouldn't let me." Fortunately, that father had not lost the war, but she said it with such intensity that I knew he would have been better off losing that battle.

We lost the battle of "sitting as a family" in church. As parents we thought it important to worship as a family, and to us that meant sitting together. We had always done so. When our children became teenagers, and many of their friends sat together, it became a real issue. After fighting it for a while, we came to a compromise. We sit as a family in the morning service, and anywhere in the evening service. We concluded that it was more important to have them in church with their friends and happy than with us and resentful.

Remember that your teenagers are adults and need to make decisions. As parents you need to let them see you make decisions, make them with you, and finally make them by themselves. If you have been teaching them how to do this as children, now is the time to begin to turn the responsibility over to them. They will make some wrong decisions. As long as these will not have lasting or devastating results, let them make them and learn from them. Of course, if they repeatedly act irresponsibly or are about to make a mistake that will leave permanent scars, step in and stop them. However, before you do, be sure the battle is worth fighting and will help you win the war.

CHAPTER THREE

Cultural and Community Identities

His parents were Danish, but before Erik was born, they separated. Erik was born near Frankfurt, Germany. Three years later his mother married Erik's Jewish pediatrician, but waited years before telling him that Dr. Homberger was not really his father. Erik considered himself German, even though his parents were Danish. However, German children rejected him because they considered him a Jew, and Jewish children rejected him because he was tall and blond.

Erik Homberger was an average student and graduated from what we would call a high school. Then he wandered around Europe for a year or so before trying an art school in Germany. After dropping out, he tried another one in Munich, then he moved to Florence, Italy. He wandered around Italy, soaking up the sun and visiting art galleries. Finally, at the age of twenty-five, he settled down to work and study.

Erik experienced many of the factors that remove identity from adolescents in our modern Western culture. He had little national identity (Danish, German, Jewish), little community identity (constant moving around), little family identity (mother divorced and remarried), and little religious identity (Jewish or Christian). It is little wonder that Erik Erikson (his biological father's name) was the one to develop the concept of the "identity crisis" during adolescence. He had experienced it himself.

Contrast Erik Homberger (Erikson?) with Jesus at the age of twelve. Mary and Joseph had taken Jesus to Jerusalem for the Passover. Thinking Jesus was with the group when they started home, they did not miss Him until the end of the day. Returning to Jerusalem, they searched three days before finding Him in the temple talking with the teachers there.

> When His parents saw Him, they were astonished. His mother said to Him, "Son, why have You treated us like this? Your father and I have been anxiously searching for You."
>
> "Why were you searching for Me?" He asked. "Didn't you know I had to be in My Father's house?'" (Luke 2:48-49)

How many twelve-year-olds today would say something like that? Probably not many, but we must remember that even though Jesus was soon going to be a teenager, He would never be an adolescent. At the age of twelve He knew who He was and much about His mission in life. Within a year, like any other twelve-year-old, He would be an adult (a teenager) and be treated as one by everyone in town.

How different this is from today's teenagers who, like Erik Erikson, often ask, "Who am I?" The reason for the difference is the invention of adolescence. Our culture today does not tell teenagers who they are. It has created adolescents without giving them an identity. Let us now consider some ways it has removed identity and some ways teenagers try to find it.

Act Your Age?

When teenagers act childish, some parents say, "Act your age," as a put-down. The problem with telling teens to act their age is that they, and we, are not sure what that means. We have removed the "rites of passage" found in "primitive" cultures. Although we often make fun of these ceremonies, they are important in giving people identities. When boys or girls begin these ceremonies, they know they will come out as men and women, even though they are still in their teens.

On the day after their thirteenth birthday Hebrew men went through their bar mitzvah, and on the day after their twelfth, women went through their bas mitzvah. These new men and women then had to keep all the commandments. They could buy and sell property. They were adults, not children, and certainly not adolescents. When a Roman boy reached his sixteenth year, he exchanged his *toga praetexta* for his *toga virilis*. From then on he would be treated as a man.

The Apostle Paul had a clear cultural identity. He wrote that he was "circumcised on the eighth day, of the people of Israel, of the tribe of Benjamin, a Hebrew of Hebrews; in regard to the law, a Pharisee" (Phil. 3:5). "Are they Hebrews? So am I. Are they Israelites? So am I. Are they Abraham's descendants? So am I" (2 Cor. 11:22). There was no question about Paul's national identity. He was a Hebrew. (He was also a Roman citizen, but he only mentioned that when he needed to.)

Of course, a ceremony itself is not important. What is important is that there be some point at which people are recognized as adults. They need to know that they are no longer children (or adolescents) and that they are full adults. Ceremonies in themselves may have little meaning.

Our culture has no "adulthood ceremony," not even an age of adulthood. Every spring high school seniors dress in long black robes and go through a ceremony in which they move some strings from one side of their heads to the other. It means they have completed high school, but it does not mean they will be treated as adults by the whole society. Half of them will go on to college and remain adolescents for several more years.

When I register at a motel, my teenagers stay free because, at the front desk, they are considered children. If we eat at the motel restaurant, they are charged adult prices because there they are considered adults. How can they "act their age" when the same institution treats them as children one hour and as adults the next?

When visiting a nearby high school, I noticed a pamphlet saying, "Passport to Adulthood." As I pulled it from the rack, I saw that it was published by the selective service system. Inside it said, "MEN: When you reach 18, you become an adult. With that new status come rewards—and responsibilities." It would be much easier for everyone if it were all that simple. Unfortunately, registering for the draft does not mean that teenagers will be treated as adults.

Do We Have to Move Again?

As a typical teenager growing up in the 1950s, I moved six times, attending five schools in four cities. Where was I from? I had little identity with any community. My teenagers have lived in the same house the last fourteen years. When we moved into it, five other boys on the block were the same age as our five-year-old son. By the time he reached high school, he was the only one left. Even when teenagers do not move, their community does.

How different from the strong community identity people had in New Testament times. In fact, we still refer to people then as being "of" a particular community.

Philip, like Andrew and Peter, was from the town of Bethsaida. Philip found Nathanael and told him, "We have found the one Moses wrote about in the Law, and about whom the prophets also wrote—Jesus of Nazareth, the son of Joseph."

"Nazareth! Can anything good come from there?" Nathanael asked.

"Come and see," said Philip. (John 1:44-46)

The Apostle Paul was also "Saul of Tarsus." When identifying himself, he said, "I am a Jew, born in Tarsus of Cilicia, but brought up in this city. Under Gamaliel I was thoroughly trained in the law of our fathers and was just as zealous for God as any of you are today" (Acts 22:3). Notice that he gives his national identity, his community identity, his religious identity, and his educational identity. We still refer to "Joseph of Arimathea" (John 19:38) and "Judas the Galilean" (Acts 5:37). The place of one's birth and residence was important.

When schools were smaller and within the neighborhood, students got a community identity from them. I began my education walking to a one-room school with kindergarten through sixth grade and one teacher. Later I went to a "city school" and graduated with about fifty in my class. I knew everyone in both schools by name. My teenagers began in an elementary school with 500 students and now attend a county high school with about 400 students in each class. They do not even know everyone in their classes, much less everyone in the school. They do not find a community identity even in their schools.

When I was bused to the city for school, it was to get a "better education." Today when people are bused, it is often to achieve racial balance. Both kinds of busing have been at the expense of a community identity for teenagers. When people first moved to the cities, they formed distinct neighborhoods. Today most of the neighborhoods are gone, and many people hardly know the names of others on the block, or even down the hall in the apartment building.

First we removed our teenagers' cultural identities by creating adolescence—we turned them into "adult-children" without telling them what they were really to be like. Then we took them from farms and small towns into large cities. We took them out of small schools in their neighborhoods and put them in huge institutions where they cannot possibly know everyone. It is little wonder that many of them ask, "Who am I?"

This Proves I'm an Adult!
In societies that have puberty rites, the young men and women have no question about when they become adults. In our society, they are never quite sure if they have arrived at adulthood or not. Are they adults when they have to pay adult prices at a restaurant, when they can get a driver's license, when they can quit school, or when they can vote? How can they prove to themselves that they are adults? What physical feat can they do to prove it? Since there are few lions or bears to slay to show that they are grown up, many look to other actions to prove their adult status.

The Twenty-sixth Amendment to the Constitution states that people can vote everywhere at age eighteen. However, the federal government is now pushing for laws in every state requiring people to be twenty-one to buy liquor. What a commentary on our culture that the final step into adulthood is the right to buy a drug that will make one irrational and irresponsible!

Many teenagers see the use of drugs as proof of their adulthood. Even though they cannot buy drugs legally, most teens use them during adolescence as a way of proving to themselves and others that they are adults. A 1982 survey by the National Institute on Drug Abuse found that nineteen out of twenty 18-to-25-year-olds had drunk alcohol. They had taken what they considered the final step in the proof of their adulthood. Furthermore, three out of four had smoked tobacco, and two out of three had used marijuana.

Several surveys have found that the majority of those who become cigarette smokers began by eighth or ninth grade. The National Youth Polydrug Study found that men first smoked marijuana at an average age of 12.8 and women at 13.1. They began drinking alcohol a little earlier. Many teenagers see the use of alcohol, tobacco, and marijuana as an initiation into adulthood. Since our culture does not have any meaningful formal rites of passage, beginning use of these drugs has become an informal rite of passage.

TEENS CREATE THEIR OWN RITES OF PASSAGE

Of course, adolescents look to other self-defined rites of passage, which we will discuss later. Some believe having sexual intercourse makes them adults. Others believe breaking a law makes them adults. They are looking for some way of proving to themselves and others that they are adults.

Do I Have to Wear That?

PEER INFLUENCE

Since adolescents do not get an identity from their culture or their community, they often turn to another group—to other teenagers. Afraid of being rejected by these other adolescents, teenagers feel a strong pressure to conform to the group. Unfortunately, those other teens do not know who they are either, so peer pressure becomes a case of "the blind leading the blind."

Teenagers pick a group they want to join, then conform to it. Such conformity shows in actions, language, beliefs, possessions, and, most obviously, in dress. There is a big difference between having a horse on your shirt and having an alligator, a fox, a

TEENS FIND GROUP FOR "IDENTIFICATION" SINCE CULTURE PROVIDES LITTLE

dragon, or a tiger. If parents suggest wearing something not "in" with the group at the moment, the suggestion will be met with, "Do I have to wear that?"

Social psychologist Solomon Asch (*Social Psychology,* Prentice-Hall) showed that adolescents conform, even to a group of strangers, on such a simple thing as judging which of two lines is longer. When making judgments alone, teens made errors about 7% of the time. When judging with a group of three or more people, they made errors about 33% of the time if the rest of the group was unanimously against them.

As the differences between the lines became less, the teenagers conformed to the group more. If they were made to feel less competent than the others in the group, they conformed even more. Unfortunately, many of the decisions adolescents make are much less clear-cut than judging the lengths of lines. Since they are also unsure of their identities, they are likely to conform to nearly anything the rest of the group does.

Further research has shown that people eleven to thirteen years of age conform more than those at any other ages. Of course, this is when they have just begun adolescence and have the least identity. They look to others to decide how to act because they do not know who they are. Since men mature later than women, we would expect the most conformity from them later. That is exactly what we find. Women conform most at twelve years of age and men at fifteen.

Pressure to conform is strong for any people not sure of their identity. The Israelites were just becoming a nation, but had judges instead of kings. The people were unhappy with Samuel's sons and asked Samuel to "appoint a king to lead us, such as all the other nations have." Samuel told the people how bad a king would be for them, "but the people refused to listen to Samuel. 'No!' they said. 'We want a king over us. Then we will be like all the other nations, with a king to lead us and to go out before us and fight our battles'" (1 Sam. 8:5, 19-20).

God knew that in asking His people to worship Him in a different way, they would feel the pressure to conform and warned them about it. "After they have been destroyed before you, be

45

careful not to be ensnared by inquiring about their gods, saying, 'How do these nations serve their gods? We will do the same' " (Deut. 12:30). He warned them not to worship God like the other nations, but it did little good. "They rejected His decrees and the covenant He had made with their fathers and the warnings He had given them. They followed worthless idols and themselves became worthless. They imitated the nations around them although the Lord had ordered them, 'Do not do as they do,' and they did the things the Lord had forbidden them to do" (2 Kings 17:15).

Such warnings are given to individuals in both the Old and New Testaments, as well as to the nation of Israel as a whole. Only a few chapters after the Ten Commandments, God said, "Do not follow the crowd in doing wrong" (Ex. 23:2). Unfortunately, teenagers may follow the crowd to take drugs, vandalize, or steal. Adolescent gangs roam the streets of our cities. Paul told the Romans, "Do not conform any longer to the pattern of this world, but be transformed by the renewing of your mind" (Rom. 12:2).

Unfortunately, conformity is not a good answer to identity, even if teens have chosen to conform to a "good" group rather than to a gang. In earlier times, people found lasting identities in their cultures and communities, but these adolescent identities are based on temporary groups. If the group rejects the adolescent, the result can be devastating. When the group breaks up, as nearly all adolescent groups finally do, the adolescent is again left without an identity.

What Can Parents Do?

Of course, as individual parents you cannot do much about the lack of cultural identity. Political action is needed to develop it, and that takes time—too much time to help your own adolescents. Furthermore, such change is unlikely to take place any time soon, even if people start taking political action. In 1985 teens spent $65 billion and any move to change adolescence would be opposed by intensive lobbying to protect the interests of those who get these billions of dollars.

Develop a "cultural identity." Just because our culture has not developed an age of adulthood does not mean that you are helpless as parents. You can develop your own "criteria of adulthood." Even though the culture itself does not tell teens what it expects, you should make it clear to your own teens what you expect of them. As we said in an earlier chapter, let them know that, even if no one else does, you expect them to act like responsible adults.

You can also have "puberty rites" for the time when your children become adolescents (adults). I know of one family who literally has a family celebration when their daughters begin menstruating. If that sounds too "primitive" to you, you could pick a *AGE 13* birthday near the age of puberty and have a "ceremony" the day each child becomes an adult in the family. Of course, you would then treat him or her as an adult from that time on.

Develop a community identity. Since part of the identity problem is that families move frequently, the solution is to stop moving. One couple, Pete and Sally, decided not to move while they had adolescents. They decided his "better" job and higher salary were not worth the cost in identity for their teenagers. Another couple, Harold and Molly, did move, but chose the new community and neighborhood with their adolescents in mind. Molly said, "The 'right' place to live for someone in Harold's position was a poor place for our teenagers. There were no other teens within five blocks."

Whether you move or not, become a part of the community. Join a church in the community. Become a part of the community choir or orchestra. Join community athletic leagues as a family. Send your children and adolescents to schools in the community. Become a part of the parent-teacher organization. Become a leader in scouts, 4-H, or other clubs where you can work together as a family.

Make your block a real neighborhood. Mike and Debbie had other families in for games and a backyard cookout. They joined a neighborhood crime-watch. They started a neighborhood Bible study group. They began walking down the street evenings, stopping to chat with people in their yards. They generally took time to be real neighbors to everyone within three or four houses.

Learn about your community. We have made it a point to subscribe to the weekly local *Jessamine Journal* as well as the daily

Lexington Herald-Leader. You can put local news clippings on a bulletin board or the refrigerator so that everyone in the family will see them. Learn about the history of your community. We were surprised, delighted, and aghast as we read the book *Wilmore, Kentucky,* and learned of the early history of our town. Although the book will never become a bestseller, it taught us much about our town.

One thing you need to do is show by your own pride and participation that you have a community identity. Some people see Wilmore as a little college town five miles from the end of the road. No one stops by just because they are passing through. One evening while giving a local teenager a ride, I asked where he planned to go to college. Though he was not sure, he said it would be somewhere other than in this "stinkin' town." I immediately knew that his parents had given him little community identity.

I later asked my son riding with me if he felt the same way about Wilmore. He said, "No, I really like living here. I have lots of friends and know everyone." We had succeeded in helping him develop a community identity. Wilmore may not be world famous, but as a family we can take pride in it. We can personally know many people in town—all the pastors, all the businessmen, both doctors, the dentist, all members of the city council, and so forth. Although we are well aware of the shortcomings of our community, we can emphasize the good things and take pride in them. Then we can work to make it better.

Any community can give teens a real role in the town. A few years ago when a teen suggested painting faces on the fire hydrants, our city council said, "We will supply the paint, if you will paint them." I know of one teenager who is planning to run for city council as soon as she turns eighteen. She knows most of the current council and feels she can have a real effect on city government, even as a teenager.

Use peer pressure. Peer pressure can be positive as well as negative, and toward Christianity as well as away from it. Mary White Harder, James Richardson, and Robert Simmonds were psychologists and sociologists at the University of Nevada when they wrote an article for *Psychology Today* on the "Jesus People" in a commune in the early 1970s. They wrote, "All of us who interviewed members came under such pressure that we felt the need to withdraw at least once a day in order to reaffirm our own world views" (December 1972, p. 113).

T. George Harris, editor of *Psychology Today* at the time, wrote, "Each time they called in after a visit, we asked them if any of them had been converted to the movement. At least one of the researchers had trouble hanging on to scientific certainty while he lived day and night among the vibrant, born-again Christians" (p. 42). The pressures were so great that even people studying the commune could hardly keep from becoming Christians.

Even a group within a group can be a positive influence. When our son Kent was in eighth grade, several Christian students started a prayer group. They gathered each morning to pray together briefly between first and second hour. After several weeks the group had grown to nearly twenty students. One afternoon Kent said, "The first teacher came to our prayer group today."

"Who was it?" I asked. When he told me, I was surprised and asked why she came.

"We were gathered in a circle praying when she pushed her way in asking, 'Who's fighting?' " said Kent. That prayer group was a source of strength that whole year, a positive peer pressure.

Even if you cannot get a group for positive peer pressure, just one other person will break the power of the group. Solomon Asch, the social psychologist who did the experiment having college students judge the lengths of lines, found that the power of the group depended on unanimity. If just one other person gave the correct answer, the pressure to conform was broken. Students then gave the correct answer, even though *nearly* everyone else was giving the incorrect one. Even Jesus sent His disciples out in pairs (Mark 6:7).

If your teenagers cannot find even one other person to stand with them, they may have to leave the group. Jeff was on the football team. Each year he found that the pressure to drink, take drugs, and listen to off-color stories dragged his Christian life down. Each summer at the Fellowship of Christian Athletes he would rededicate his life, then go through the same cycle again. Finally, he

49

made the very difficult choice to quit the team.

Although you alone cannot change the culture, you can go a long way toward giving your teen a community identity. The major factor is your own attitude. If you do not have a community identity with pride in your community, you will not be able to pass this on to your adolescents. You can also help your teens find a good group so they will feel positive pressures to conform. As parents of teenagers, we need to help make good things happen in our teenagers' lives.

CHAPTER FOUR

Family and Sexual Identities

Scott and Jennifer were on their first date since meeting two weeks before when they arrived at college. Trying to make small talk to get acquainted, Scott asked, "Jennifer, where does your dad work?"

Hesitating a bit, Jennifer said, "Which one?" Her parents had divorced, and her mother had remarried.

A few minutes later Jennifer asked Scott, "Where do your parents live?"

"New York and Florida," he replied. His parents had divorced and lived in different states. Questions about an adolescent's family are no longer small talk. They often strike painfully at the teenager's struggle with identity. Not only have we removed cultural and community identity, but we have also removed family identity.

Roots?
In the past, teenagers had strong family identities as well as cultural and community identities. In New Testament times the father's name became a part of the son's. "Then he brought Simon to Jesus, who looked at him and said, 'You are Simon son of John. You will be called Cephas' (which, when translated, is Peter)"

51

(John 1:42). Even later, when Jesus knew him well, He still addressed him using a variation of his father's name. "Jesus replied, 'Blessed are you, Simon son of Jonah, for this was not revealed to you by man, but by My Father in heaven' " (Matt. 16:17).

Sometimes we know the father's name, but not the child's. "Then they came to Jericho. As Jesus and His disciples, together with a large crowd, were leaving the city, a blind man, Bartimaeus (that is the son of Timaeus), was sitting by the roadside begging" (Mark 10:46). All we know about the identity of "Blind Bartimaeus" is that he was the son of a man named Timaeus.

The family identity was not limited to the immediate family, but tied in with the cultural and community identity. When Philip first told Nathanael about Jesus, he called Him, "Jesus of Nazareth, the son of Joseph" (John 1:45). Bartimaeus also tied these identities together. "When he heard that it was Jesus of Nazareth, he began to shout, 'Jesus, Son of David, have mercy on me!' " (Mark 10:47) Jesus was from Nazareth, and He was the son of David.

We often skip rapidly over the genealogies in Scripture such as those found in Genesis 5, 10, and 11, Matthew 1, and Luke 3. We may think it odd that the book of Ruth ends with a genealogy. However, genealogies similar to these could be given by most Hebrews in Jesus' day. They were a vital part of a person's family identity.

Jews referred to themselves as children of their father Abraham (John 8:31-41). Their family identities were also tied in with their national and religious identities. God was not only an infinite, all-powerful being who had saved them, but He had also said, "I am the God of your fathers, the God of Abraham, Isaac and Jacob" (Acts 7:32). The Apostle Paul said, "I am an Israelite myself, a descendant of Abraham, from the tribe of Benjamin" (Rom. 11:1). His family identity was tied into his national identity. Every Hebrew could tell you the tribe (family) from which he or she had descended.

Today, with our emphasis on individuality and making it on our own, we look at these family identities as being rather odd. Even the nineteenth-century feud between the Hatfields and the McCoys in our own country seems rather quaint. We cannot imagine doing something, especially hurting someone, just because they have a particular last name. Most adolescents receive little family identity and know little about their families before their grandparents or great-grandparents. Let us consider some of the factors which have led to this loss of family identity.

Divorce is common and many adolescents do not even want to claim one side of their families. At the turn of the century there was one divorce for every thirteen marriages. Although the marriage rate stayed about the same, divorce increased so that by the mid 1970s there was one divorce for every two marriages. In earlier times even when there was discord, parents often waited until their children left home to divorce, if they divorced at all. That may have done other damage to teenagers, but at least they had a better chance to develop family identities.

Today's typical divorce leaves the mother with the children, and she usually remarries. This further adds to the identity problems of adolescents because then they are not even sure of their names. Their last names become different from those of their parents (mother and stepfather). Having the stepfather legally adopt them is of little help in achieving a family identity, because then they have to change even their name, their whole identity. I know of several homes where the children have three different last names and are struggling with their identities.

During the last few years more women have been keeping their maiden names when they marry. Their children have to struggle with their family name when they become adolescents because our society does not tell them which name to use. As more unmarried couples live together and have children, their adolescents face the same problem, lack of a family name.

As illegitimacy rises, more adolescents face identity problems. More unmarried women are becoming pregnant, and more of them are refusing to marry the father of the child. By 1983 one child in five born in the United States had no legal father. In some large cities more than half the children born have none. We refer to these as "illegitimate children," but it is really the parents who are illegitimate. Illegitimate literally means "not lawful," and it is the parents who are not legally married. When these children become adolescents, they face identity problems.

Today about one person in five under eighteen years of age lives in a single-parent home at any one time. That may seem like a small percentage, but we are talking about nearly thirteen *million* people who are struggling with an added problem in their search for identity. In fact, before they leave home, about three out of five will live for a while in a single-parent home. Adolescents who had their cultural identity removed with the invention of adolescence and their community identity removed with the move to the cities are now having their family identities removed with the breakdown of the family.

Some teens try to find family identity by creating it themselves. Some, dissatisfied with their own families, marry to become someone's husband or wife. They marry to escape, but usually end up creating a new family much like the one they left. Others have a baby to answer their identity problem. They become somebody's mother. Of course, these are not adequate solutions.

What Is a Woman? A Man?

At one time men and women were culturally distinctly different. The Apostle Paul said, "Does not the very nature of things teach you that if a man has long hair, it is a disgrace to him, but that if a woman has long hair, it is her glory? For long hair is given to her as a covering" (1 Cor. 11:14-15). Although we may argue that these differences are not instinctive, at least hair length once served as an indicator of sexual identity.

Paul insisted on men and women dressing differently for worship. "Every many who prays or prophesies with his head covered dishonors his head. And every woman who prays or prophesies with her head uncovered dishonors her head—it is just as though her head were shaved" (1 Cor. 11:4-5). Men and women dressed differently as well as cut their hair differently.

Such distinctions have gradually disappeared. In most races after puberty hair grows on men's faces, but not on women's. Beards distinguish men from boys—and men from women. In our culture, men usually shave off their beards, making them look more like women. Of course, a beard itself does not make a person a man, but it is one natural way men are different from women.

Men and women in our society used to dress differently. Today most adolescents dress alike. Both male and female teenagers wear blue jeans, a shirt, and tennis shoes. Teachers may have difficulty telling whether students are men or women. I know a sixth-grade teacher who has finally found a good method for making that distinction at school during those first few days before he learns who is who. He watches which rest room they use!

In high school women were once expected to take home economics and think about becoming homemakers, nurses, or teachers. Men took shop and thought about becoming truck drivers, coal miners, and business executives. Today a woman who chooses to be a homemaker may be criticized by other women for settling for tradition. Men are told to consider being nurses, telephone operators, and househusbands (while their wives work outside the home).

By the mid 1970s, we were told that androgyny was best. That is, an individual was to have both masculine (andro) and feminine (gyn) qualities. Psychologist Sandra Bem concluded that the androgynous were healthiest psychologically, and the others had problems. The ones with the worst problems were the feminine females.

After removing the adolescents' cultural, community, family, and sexual identities, our culture tells them, "Be yourselves." Or it says, "Do your own thing." Unfortunately, adolescents do not know who they are or what "their thing" is. They are confused and have little identity.

I Won't!
Some teens try to find their identities by doing the opposite of what their parents and others in authority want them to do. This rejection of authority becomes a new, negative identity.

If parents ask adolescents to wear their hair short, they wear it long. If parents favor long hair, adolescents cut it short. They become atheists, agnostics, or members of another religion if their parents want them to be Christians. They become Methodists if the parents are Baptists, or Baptists if the parents are Methodists. Young men grow beards when parents want them to shave, and shave when parents want them to grow beards.

If the school administration has a dress code, these adolescents want to wear something else. If there is no dress code, they all dress alike. Blue jeans have almost become a high school uniform, but if the administration said that all students had to wear denim, those adolescents with a negative identity would insist on wearing something else. Since teachers want them to study, they refuse to do it, even if the material interests them.

In the late 1960s the college where I was teaching passed a rule that students could not wear blue jeans in the dining room. Anyone who came to the door in them would not be admitted, but would have to eat a sack lunch outside. Students suddenly started showing up at the dining hall in blue jeans and sat around the door singing "We Shall Overcome" and other freedom songs. That it was a negative identity for some was evident from the fact that they had to buy blue jeans to wear because they did not have any when the rule was passed.

The problem with a negative identity, like that with conformity, is that it is not a lasting identity. This identity also comes only from others. When adolescents leave home and school, they have no identity. Though they would not admit it, their identity has come from parents and school administrators.

Furthermore, a negative identity simply does not work in adult life. If an employer requires employees to wear suits or dresses and the employees insist on blue jeans, they lose their jobs. Adolescents can use a negative identity because we do not expect them to act like adults. They do not have to worry about losing their jobs or being arrested. They do not have to work, and juvenile courts take care of them if they become delinquent. Other adults cannot live in our society using only a negative identity.

I Will!

Other teens try to find their identities by doing the opposite, by being very obedient to authorities. They try to please the authority and will do almost anything. They may obey their parents, their teachers—or their gang leaders. They may worship, study, or steal, each because they are obeying some authority.

Although we may not think of adolescents as obedient, the fact is that many of them, like other adults, are very obedient to authority. Psychologist Stanley Milgram did a long series of experiments in the 1960s and early 1970s. In the studies, college students were asked to help "conduct experiments" on the effect of punishment on learning. When the "learner" made an error, the student was to give him an electric shock. The shocks grew stronger each time the learner erred.

The apparatus showed the shocks as becoming more and more dangerous. The "learner" never actually received any shocks, but acted as if they were becoming more and more painful. The object of the experiments was to see how far the student would go in obeying the experimenter, even when the learner was screaming in pain (Stanley Milgram, *Obedience to Authority,* Harper & Row).

He found that about three out of five college students would obey the experimenter to the end, even when they thought that they were really hurting someone else. Notice that he did his experiments during the days when college students were anything but docile. At that time in our history they were rioting on college campuses, and people thought they were very disobedient.

Two other psychologists asked students (one at a time) at Princeton Theological Seminary to give a speech about the Good Samaritan. Some were told that they were early for their talk. Others were told they were late, so they would have to hurry. As students entered the building where they were to give the speech, they found someone slumped in the doorway asking for help. About two-thirds of those who were early stopped to help, but only one in ten who was late stopped. In their obedience to the experimenter, those seminary students literally stepped over someone in need while on their way to talk about the Good Samaritan (John Darley and Daniel Batson, " 'From Jerusalem to Jericho': A Study of Situational and Dispositional Variables in Helping Behavior," *Journal of Personality and Social Psychology,* 1973, *27,* pp. 100-108).

The problem with obedience, like that of conformity and negative identity, is that it is no identity at all. Identity comes from others because all the adolescent is doing is what those others say. Obedience is usually more socially acceptable than conformity or a negative identity. In fact, obedience will allow even adults to get along in society, but it does not bring satisfaction. Such obedient people are frustrated because they cannot please everyone all the time.

What Can Parents Do?

Just as you can take steps to give your teenagers a community identity and take advantage of pressures toward conformity, so you can do something about family and sexual identities.

Develop a family identity. If anyone is going to give adolescents a strong sense of family identity, it will have to be you as parents. However, you first need to be sure of your own sense of family identity. You cannot give your teenagers an identity you do not have. The most important things you can do are to maintain a strong marriage and to show your adolescents where they fit into your immediate family.

As parents you have the responsibility for family stability. Strong marriages take effort on the part of both husband and wife. Separation and divorce can be avoided only if both really work to make the marriage succeed. Arguing brings fear to adolescents, even in strong families. They see their friends' parents divorcing and think that is what is going to happen in their own families. This does not mean that parents can never disagree, but when they do, it must always be clear to the teenager that divorce is not even an option.

Although the situation is not ideal, single parents can do much to give their adolescents family identities. Divorce and remarriage make the problem more difficult, but they do not make identity impossible. The following suggestions can be used by single parents as well as by two-parent families.

If you do not already know your roots, trace your family tree. The records in your county courthouse may yield many surprises. Find the origin of your family name. Ask grandparents and great-grandparents to remember everything they can about the family history and write it down. It will be valuable to pass on to your grandchildren in a few years.

Get together with living relatives. If possible see that your adolescents spend time with their grandparents and great-grandparents. If they are far away, have them write or phone. Attend family reunions. I remember many annual picnic reunions under the trees on July 4 with scores of aunts, uncles, and cousins I hardly knew. If you have given family names as middle names or as first names, make sure your teens realize it. Point out characteristics of their grandparents, aunts, and uncles in your adolescents. Help them see that they are part of a larger family.

Pass on family traditions, or begin them if the family has few. Family devotions, holiday activities, vacations, and annual weekends are all examples of family activities that become traditions. Reading the Christmas story from the Bible is a tradition in many homes. Hand down family heirlooms. I slept in the same crib as my father, then a few years ago our infants slept in it, and we hope our grandchildren will do the same. Teenagers should see their names appearing in a family Bible handed down from generation to generation to give them a sense of where they belong in the family. If one was not given to you, start one. Take a family picture every year. Since I have moved from my childhood home, last summer we took our teens back to visit places important to me as I grew up.

Take time to be a family. You cannot develop a family identity if you are never together. Norton and Celeste both went to work every day, and in the evening they were too tired to spend time doing things with their children and adolescents. They finally decided that Saturday was to be their family day and refused all other Saturday activities for several years.

Doug and Gail were so involved in church and community activities that they were building no family identity. Although their friends were quite critical, they resigned from several organizations and committees to spend time with their families. We often hear that the quantity of time is not important, but the quality is. Both are important—no one can build a strong family identity on only ten minutes a day together.

Parents can also give adolescents a real role in the family. Teenagers were expected to work as a part of the family before adolescence was invented. They still need to wash, cook, clean, rake, mow, weed, and do any other necessary tasks at home. Too often they feel unneeded at home, not really part of the family. Rather than being boarders or guests, they should be participating members of the family group. Family meetings with everyone participating, one meal a day with every member of the family present, and everyone going to concerts or plays in which a member of the family is involved are good. Family nights once a week are effective too. However, these activities become more difficult as adolescents grow older.

Develop a sexual identity. To help your teens develop sexual identities, the first thing you need is to be sure of your own sexuality. You cannot help your teens define their sexual identity if you are not confident of your own. "So God created man in His own image, in the image of God He created him; male and female He created them" (Gen. 1:27). Your very sexuality is part of the image of God in you. Although our society today wants to make men and women the same, they are different. From birth boys and girls have differences in their brains, their activity levels, and so forth. As we saw in chapter 1, men reach puberty later than women.

The Bible talks about being fathers and mothers, another part of our sexual identity. Of course, as you read these passages, you must remember that the Bible is talking about being mothers and fathers to children, not adolescents (Eph. 6:1-4; Deut. 6). People in Bible times treated their teenagers as adults, and I believe we should too. Of course, we do need to be fathers and mothers to children in the home, and make a distinction in our behavior toward children and adolescents.

The Bible also talks about being husbands and wives, another aspect of our sexual identity. Parents need to be role models for their adolescents this way too. The New Testament gives clear instructions for husbands, wives, and children. Husbands and wives need to read these, considering entire passages, not just looking at isolated verses.

Ralph had always quoted Ephesians 5:22 to Crystal, "Wives, submit to your husbands as to the Lord." While in a Bible study on Ephesians, he outlined the whole book. He outlined the end of chapter 5 and beginning of chapter 6 as follows:

I. Submit to one another (5:21–6:9)
   A. How wives submit (5:22-24)
   B. How husbands submit (5:25-33)
   C. How children submit (6:1-3)
   D. How fathers submit (6:4)
   E. How slaves submit (6:5-8)
   F. How masters submit (6:9)

Then he compared the passage with 1 Peter 3:1-7. Finally, he made practical application to his own life. He realized that as a husband and father he had fallen short, and he began to live his life the way Peter and Paul suggested. Even his teenagers noticed the change in his life.

Compliment adolescents on being "young men" and "young women." Even if you wanted a child of the opposite sex, do not try to remake the one you have. Attend father-son and mother-daughter events. Discuss television shows, especially the situation comedies that give a false impression of our sexual identities. Many current television shows portray parents as fools, markedly different from the days of "Father Knows Best." Do not make sarcastic remarks or jokes putting down the opposite sex. Popular "women driver" jokes and "mother-in-law" jokes usually do that.

Warn your teenagers about their tendency to develop a negative identity and their tendency to obey. Simply being aware of these tendencies can help all of us avoid them. Encourage your teens to think things through, rather than simply obeying or refusing to obey. Remind them that they have a new capacity for thinking and help them use it.

Let us not simply turn our adolescents loose in a world that gives them little identity. As parents, we can at least give them a family identity and a sexual identity, along with their community identity. This identity came easily and naturally in normal life before the creation of adolescence. Today we have to consciously work at developing it.

CHAPTER FIVE

Isn't God the Answer?

Gert and Chuck were eating pizza in the corner booth when she looked out the window and saw a bumper sticker that read, "Christ is the answer." Turning to Chuck, Gert said, "When I began to ask who I was and to question the purpose of my life, I thought God was the answer. I went to Mom and Dad's church, but the people there and the pastor did not even seem to understand my questions. They were saying nice things, but I didn't find any real answers there."

Chuck replied, "My folks didn't go to church, but I kept hearing about being 'born again' from some friends. I tried it, and for a while I thought I had some answers. When I was still unsatisfied, I joined a cult and lived in it for about a year and a half. I realized that they didn't have any real answers either, so I left."

Chuck and Gert are talking about the loss of another kind of identity. Not only have adolescents lost their cultural, community, family, and sexual identities, but they have also lost their religious identity. Let us look at what has happened.

They Knew Who They Were!
At one time belonging to a culture, a community, and a family meant that you automatically received a religious identity. The

same word could mean either a culture or a religion. A Jew was one who was a descendant of Abraham or someone whose religion was Judaism. Teenage Jews in Old or New Testament times did not have to decide what religion they would be. They knew who they were.

The Israelites knew they were God's chosen people from the time of the writing of the Books of Moses. "For you are a people holy to the Lord your God. Out of all the people on the face of the earth, the Lord has chosen you to be His treasured possession" (Deut. 14:2). New Testament Christians had the same concept. The Apostle Paul said, "For He chose us in Him before the creation of the world to be holy and blameless in His sight" (Eph. 1:4). "But you are a chosen people, a royal priesthood, a holy nation, a people belonging to God, that you may declare the praises of Him who called you out of darkness into His wonderful light" (1 Peter 2:9).

This is sometimes expressed as the concept of election. Jesus said, "And He will send His angels with a loud trumpet call, and they will gather His elect from the four winds, from one end of the heavens to the other" (Matt. 24:31). Paul said, "Therefore I endure everything for the sake of the elect, that they too may obtain the salvation that is in Christ Jesus, with eternal glory" (2 Tim. 2:10).

Closely tied to the concept of being chosen is that of being children of God, a family identity. Look at the verses just before and after the first two considered above. "You are the children of the Lord your God" (Deut. 14:1). "He predestined us to be adopted as His sons through Jesus Christ, in accordance with His pleasure and will" (Eph. 1:5). They were not only children of Abraham and children of Israel, they were also children of God Himself.

Those who are led by the Spirit of God are sons of God. For you did not receive a spirit that makes you a slave again to fear, but you received the Spirit of sonship. And by Him we cry, "*Abba*, Father." The Spirit Himself testifies with our spirit that we are God's children. Now if we are children, then we are heirs—heirs of God and co-heirs with Christ, if indeed we share in His sufferings in order that we may also share in His glory. (Rom. 8:14-17)

Both their cultural and family identities were tied in with their religious identity. As a nation the Israelites were waiting for the Messiah. Notice the "family" words in Paul's letter to the Romans: sons, sonship, father, children, and heirs. The Jews before Christ and the Christians after Him both knew their religious identity. They were God's children.

Where Do We Fit?

Few adolescent Christians in our culture have the same sense of religious identity. They do not have a feeling of where they fit in God's plan for the redemption of the world. They are not waiting for the Messiah, and many feel no call to tell others that He has come. Their religious identity is separated from their national and family identities.

Some countries have a state religion. If the government supports a particular church and most of the people belong to it, teenagers get their religious identity without having to think much about it. From its beginning, the United States separated church and state. The First Amendment to the Constitution states, "Congress shall make no law respecting an establishment of religion, or prohibiting the free exercise thereof." Although we prize this freedom, it means that our adolescents struggle with their religious identity.

With this freedom, adolescents have to decide whether to be Christian, Muslim, Buddhist, Hindu, or some other religion. If they pick Christianity, they can be Roman Catholic or Protestant. If they pick Protestant, they can be Baptist, Methodist, Presbyterian, Assembly of God, or a variety of others. Even within these denominations is an amazing variety. In our town of 3500 people we have two varieties of Baptist churches and two of Methodist.

Even belonging to a church gives little identity. Many mainline churches decided that to minister to more people they had to be pluralistic. They now present a smorgasbord of beliefs and values, and people are free to pick the ones they like best. Rather than saying that one way is right, such churches say that many ways are—just pick one you like. When I hear that someone is a United Methodist, that tells me little about what she believes or how she lives. Membership in most churches gives little religious identity. Members of different churches may look and act alike—and like people who are not members of any church.

I Thought It Would All Be Different!

Some adolescents try to find their religious identity through religious conversion. Preachers tell them that if they are "born again," they will be totally new. They seem to believe that a conversion experience will give them not only a religious identity, but cultural, community, and family identities as well. The church refers to itself as a community of believers in the family of God.

At about the turn of the century Edwin Starbuck published his classic on the psychology of religion. In his chapter on conversion he noted that it was nearly always between the ages of ten and twenty-five. That is, *"conversion is a distinctively adolescent phenomenon"* (*The Psychology of Religion*, Scribner, p. 28, italics his). He even found that conversions in women averaged about two years earlier than those in men. Religious conversion usually occurred at about the age of puberty, when people have the greatest identity problems.

Between 1899 and 1916 the average age for conversion and church membership was sixteen. At the turn of the century conversion, baptism, and church membership were seen as adult experiences. By 1955, the average had gradually lowered to a little over twelve. Of course, from chapter 1 we know that the age of adulthood (puberty) has decreased from about sixteen to about twelve, so conversion is still really an adult experience. The problem is that we now consider teenagers to be children (adolescents), not adults.

Some adolescents actually have a conversion experience. They are really "born again" and become "new creatures in Christ" (John 3:1-8; 2 Cor. 5:16-21). However, though they are children of God, they do not feel like it. Because they do not have a strong family identity in our culture, they have a "sense of identity" problem in being a part of the family of God. Since they do not know what it feels like to be part of a human family, they have difficulty feeling as though they belong to the family of God. They may have a hard time praying, "Our Father in heaven," or feeling that they are "brothers and sisters" in Christ.

The lost son in Jesus' parable had this sense-of-identity problem. "I will set out and go back to my father and say to him: Father, I have sinned against heaven and against you. I am no longer worthy to be called your son; make me like one of your hired men" (Luke 15:18-19). Of course, even though he did not feel like a son, that did not change the fact of his sonship, as shown by the reaction of his father when he returned home. His father ignored his feelings of a lack of family identity and treated him for what he was, a son.

Others try Christianity as a means of finding identity, but never develop a relationship with Christ Himself. Still others join a church because it is the "in" thing to do in their group (conformity), because Mom and Dad want them to (obedience), or because Mom and Dad do not want them to (negativism). All of these are likely to be disappointed and drop out. Conversion, baptism, and church membership give adolescents a religious identity, but not a cultural, community, or family one. Most teenagers expect more than a religious identity. When they do not find it, they quit.

One day while standing in the hall of our church, I noticed a map of the Sunday School rooms. The map had two fourth-grade classes, two fifth-grade classes, two sixth-grade classes—then the decline started. It had one seventh-grade class, one class for eighth and ninth graders; one class for tenth, eleventh, and twelfth graders; and one class for college students (all four years of college). In general, attendance at Sunday School peaks at about eleven or twelve years of age, then drops rapidly during the junior high years, and even more during high school.

They Know What They Believe!
Each year thousands of adolescents, disappointed at not finding identity in their churches, join cults. Ron Enroth has studied cults for many years and has said that probably more than anything else, young people joining cults are searching for identity and

spiritual reality. Cults promise a strong identity, a challenge, and answers to the adolescent's questions. Adolescents want answers. Even if the answers are wrong, they still want answers.

Most of those joining cults are from eighteen to twenty-two years of age—late adolescents. They are usually white, middle class, have some college education and a nominally religious background. That is, they are average American adolescents. The cults have much in common with evangelical Christianity and are often attractive to young evangelicals.

Jim Jones, founder of the doomed People's Temple, was converted in a Church of the Nazarene. Moses David, founder of the Children of God, had a Christian and Missionary Alliance background. Victor Paul Wierwille, founder of The Way, was a Reformed pastor at one time. Such cults often not only have doctrines similar to those found in evangelical Christianity, but they also provide an identity not offered by established churches.

Psychiatrist Saul Levine has thoroughly studied more than 800 "radical departures" in fifteen different cults. Radical departures are young people who abruptly turn their backs on family and friends to join a cult. They have appeared to be normal American adolescents. Suddenly they leave to join a commune and break all relationships with their families and churches. Although these cults seem to offer an identity, it is not lasting, and more than nine out of ten radical departures return home within two years. In fact, nearly all ultimately return when they find that the cult does not give the the lasting identity they are seeking (*Radical Departures*, Harcourt Brace Jovanovich).

What Can Parents Do?

As in all other types of identity, your first responsibility is to be sure of your own religious identity. You may not be able to lead your teenagers to a primary experience with God because you do not have such an experience yourselves. You may have considered your own parents fanatics and have adopted a more "respectable" religious position. Now you are unable to pass much of a religious identity on to your adolescents. If this is the case, your first step is to clear up your own relationship with God.

Involve teenagers in today's church. You need to settle in one church and stay there. It is difficult for anyone to develop a religious identity moving from church to church every few months. The search for a "perfect church" is never ending and leads to a lack of religious identity. A church in your community where other members of your family go combines a religious identity with family and community identities.

You should have a justifiable pride in your religion, your denomination, and your local church. Be participating members, and be careful of criticisms you make. See yourselves as part of God's plan to redeem the world. Tom and Helen sent their teenagers to Sunday School but did not attend themselves. They refused to serve on the church board because "the 'inner circle' runs everything anyway." They never attended Sunday evening or midweek services. Then they could not understand why their teens dropped out and did not try to find their identity in the same church, with the same God. It was obvious to everyone else why their teens had left.

Teenagers also need to have a real role in the church. As parents, encourage them to be on committees, commissions, boards, and so forth. If your church does not have adolescent members in such groups, try to bring changes in the church. These groups should have adolescent members with full votes and full responsibility to work. Teenagers should sing in the choir with other members, usher with other adults, teach Sunday School classes, work in the church library, and generally participate in every part of church life.

They may not be experienced enough to do some of these things alone, but they can work on a team and learn from others. At the age of fifteen Bert was chairman of the Prayer Meeting Committee. His committee of six had full responsibility for conducting the midweek service. Adolescents can often serve as short-term missionaries, where they function as adults. Remember that at thirteen Jesus, like other Jewish men, began participating as an adult in Judaism. He read the Torah in the synagogue.

The church should distinguish between adults and children, and treat adolescents as adults. Baptism, communion, confirmation, church membership and similar activities should be seen as adult rituals. If infants and children participate in these, such as in infant baptism, there should be other rituals for adults in the church. We always told our children that communion was for adults who had been born again and asked that they not take it until then.

Teach teenagers about yesterday's church. Learn about the history of Christianity, your denomination, and your local church. Some parts of it will be sources of pride to you, and other parts will bring shame. Begin with the Bible, which gives some excellent suggestions to you as parents.

> In the future, when your son asks you, "What is the meaning of the stipulations, decrees and laws the Lord our God has commanded you?" tell him: "We were slaves of Pharaoh in Egypt, but the Lord brought us out of Egypt with a mighty hand. Before our eyes the Lord sent miraculous signs and wonders—great and terrible—upon Egypt and Pharaoh and his whole household. But He brought us out from there to bring us in and give us the land that He promised on oath to our forefathers. (Deut. 6:20-23)

The Old and New Testaments tell the story of the development of Judaism and early Christianity. Go beyond that and look at the church during the Middle Ages and the Reformation. Notice that Moses suggested this approach to teaching about the commands of God. Rather than teach God's laws with a "because God said so" attitude, show how they fit into God's plan for humanity.

Study the history of the development of your own denomination. When looking at that, we tied it to our own family history, combining a family identity with a religious one. We received a pleasant surprise and more of a feeling of identity than we expected. I could remember relatives of my grandparents' generation (born in the nineteenth century) talking about our forefathers being followers of John Huss in Bohemia. They were driven out of Bohemia because of religious persecution, finally coming to America from Germany.

They seemed to be proud of this, but I thought it was silly as a child and teenager. All I knew about Bohemia then was that beer bottles often called their contents "Bohemian Beer." Bohemians seemed to be known more for their riotous living than for their piety. When our children became teenagers, we looked up John Huss and his followers, the Hussites. We traced their history without really expecting to find much of relevance to us, but were excited at what we found.

After Huss was burned at the stake in 1415, his followers became the Bohemian Brethren. Religious persecution followed, so they moved to neighboring Moravia and became the Moravian Brethren and finally the Moravian church. After moving to Germany, the Moravians had a profound influence on the religious development of John Wesley, who founded the Methodist church to which our family now belongs. Thus, we were able to tie family and religious identities closely together. You may be just as surprised at what you find in the history of your family and church.

While studying the history of our local church, we found that it began exactly a hundred years after the beginning of American Methodism. Our church celebrated its centennial the same year that Methodism celebrated its bicentennial. Your adolescents need to see themselves as a part of this history and as making history in the plans they are originating and carrying out in their own church and denomination.

Involve teenagers in "the church in the home." Adolescents need to be given a real role in the religious life of the home. They should have a part in family devotions. Too often these devotions become miniature church services with parents performing and teenagers observing. Teens need to be involved in every aspect of home worship, from reading the Bible to commenting on it to praying and singing. Each adolescent should have his or her own Bible and participate fully in family Bible studies or small group Bible studies in the church.

Of course, if adolescents do not carry out their responsibilities as adults, they should be replaced as other adults would be. If they act like children, they should be treated as such until they act like adults. Be careful not to expect more out of them than you would other adults. Remember that all adults make mistakes and have poor judgment occasionally. However, when teenagers are worse than other adults, they should be removed from their positions of responsibility.

Expect your adolescents to have doubts about their religion. Do not throw up your hands in despair when they ask difficult questions about the church. Remember that this is the first time in their lives they can think abstractly. Just as they are critical of you and of their culture, they are critical of their religion. They can imagine the perfect church and begin to see inconsistencies in their own church and perhaps its doctrines. They can imagine the perfect Christian and begin to think that people in their church are hypocrites. Their idealism is carried into the church.

✳ Although this may sound odd, see that your adolescents do not expect too much of their religion. In Jesus' time Judaism provided people with cultural and family identities. Christianity today does not. Adolescents can be biblical Christians with Christian worldviews and have little cultural or family identity. Remember that the Bible does not deal with adolescence, and theologians have not developed a theology of adolescence. Your adolescents must realize that their religious identity is only a religious one, not a complete identity.

Study cults. Of course, you are responsible for the entire Christian education of your children and adolescents, but learning about cults is especially important during adolescence. Since so many of the cults are very similar in doctrine to basic Christianity, your teenagers need to know the difference between basic historic doctrines of the church and the heresies of the cults.

As Todd was getting into his car at the mall, two "Moonies" approached him. He talked with them and was impressed with their sense of mission and commitment. He mentioned it at dinner that evening. Rather than giving a stern warning about cults, Todd's parents encouraged Todd and his sister to join them in a study of the Unification Church. Within a couple of weeks the teenagers understood the Moonies better and were not nearly as impressed as Todd had been at first.

Parents of radical departures face very difficult decisions. "Deprogrammers" have received much publicity and parents may be tempted to use them. As noted above, more than nine out of ten radical departures leave the cult within two years, and almost all leave the group eventually. The best course for parents seems to be to "watch and pray." Not only is kidnapping illegal, but it may also cause more harm than good.

This chapter finishes the part on loss of identity. We have created adolescence without giving adolescents a clear statement about what is expected of them. At the same time we have removed community, family, sexual, and religious identities. We should not be surprised that they do not know who they are. We do not know who they are either.

As parents, our responsibility is to help them achieve a stable identity in our communities, our families, and our churches. They must see themselves as a part of society, not just as surplus people putting in time until society can absorb them.

C H A P T E R   S I X

It's Not Fair!

As Pat and Lynne came into the house, Pat was smacking his lips saying, "Lynne, this candy bar is delicious. Too bad you can't have one."

Five-year-old Lynne broke into tears and said, "It's not fair. I should have some candy too."

In the kitchen, Mom heard the whole thing. "Pat, you're fourteen and can mow lawns to earn money for candy. It would be best if you would share with Lynne. If you're going to eat it without giving her any, at least don't tease her with it. She's right—it's not fair for you to enjoy it and tell her how good it is if she can't have any."

Most of us would probably agree with what that mother said. We have a sense of fairness and would tell our children the same thing. But we do to our adolescents what Pat was doing to Lynne. We tell them how wonderful sex is and then tell them they cannot have any. This was not the situation as adolescence was being created. People then did not talk publicly about how good sex was.

The Joy of Sex
During the last half of the twentieth century we have made sex a topic of open discussion. Producers openly portray it in X- and R-

rated movies and strongly imply it in PG-rated movies, especially those rated PG-13. Teens can find it not only in hard-core pornographic magazines, but in magazines at the checkout counter of the supermarket.

They also find it not only in novels, but also in nonfiction books. *The Joy of Sex* became a bestseller and was soon followed by *More Joy of Sex.* Then came *The Joy of Gay Sex* and *The Joy of Lesbian Sex.* Children and adolescents do not even have to be able to read to get in on the current discussions of sex. Anyone who can turn on a television set can hear nearly any sexual topic discussed.

By 1970 Christians too talked openly about sex. In *The Christian Family,* Larry Christenson asked, "Isn't there anybody around to say that sex is *fun?*" (Bethany, p. 22, italics his) In his pastoral advice to teens in *The Stork Is Dead,* Charlie Shedd asserted, "*Sex is one of life's most positive positives*" (Word, p. 87, italics his). Almost a quarter of *The Total Woman* was devoted to sex, and that section ended with a chapter entitled, "Super Sex." Other books had titles like *Christian: Celebrate Your Sexuality, Intended for Pleasure,* and *Celebration in the Bedroom.*

Today's Christians point out that the Bible has many positive things to say about sex. Sex is not only for procreation and communication, but also for recreation. It is to be fun and to feel good. The Song of Solomon is dedicated to the joy of sexual love. In it both women and men are portrayed as enjoying sex greatly.

Referring to sexual intercourse with one's wife, Proverbs says, "Let thy fountain be blessed: and rejoice with the wife of thy youth. Let her be as the loving hind and pleasant roe; let her breasts satisfy thee at all times; and be thou ravished always with her love" (Prov. 5:18-19, KJV). That is restrained King James English. Some modern translations are even more graphic.

You Can't Have Any!

At the same time we tell adolescents how wonderful sex is, we tell them they they cannot marry and have any. This is no problem for some people. Sex researcher Alfred Kinsey found that about 3% of men under thirty-one reported frequencies of orgasm from zero to once in ten weeks for any five-year period. Other research has shown that perhaps about one man in five and a larger percentage of women have little interest in sex. These individuals are happy, successful in their work, and are liked by their families. Sexual abstinence is certainly a valid option for a full life.

However, many individuals do not find this suitable. When Alfred Kinsey published his *Sexual Behavior in the Human Male* (Saunders) in 1948, people were shocked at the amount of adolescent sexual activity he reported. It was far more than most people had imagined. Regardless of the laws our legislators pass, adolescents are not nonsexual beings. They are adults with adult sexual desires. In fact, the adolescent years are the times of greatest sexual desire for some people, especially men.

Kinsey found the age of maximum sexual activity in men to be somewhere between sixteen and twenty years of age. The greatest number of "sexual outlets" (orgasms) occurred at about sixteen or seventeen in both married and unmarried men. If we assume that the fathers of these adolescents were between forty-one and forty-five years old, single adolescent men averaged nearly 70% *more* orgasms each week than their married fathers.

Not only was the total number of orgasms greatest during adolescence, but so was the number of sources of orgasm, such as intercourse, masturbation, nocturnal emissions, homosexual contacts, animal contacts, and so forth. The greatest average number of sources occurred between sixteen and twenty years of age. Among the younger-maturing men, 99.5% had a regular sexual outlet by the age of fifteen.

Passing laws to prohibit marriage simply did not stop sexual activity. God created us as sexual beings (male and female) in His image, and cultural restrictions do not abolish our sexuality. The fact is that the time of greatest sexual activity in males occurs shortly after puberty. Since our culture does not allow adolescents to marry and have sexual intercourse in marriage, they find other ways to express their sexuality. In fact, only a small percentage of either men or women have their first sexual orgasm in marriage.

Our secular culture has faced the problem of sexual frustration during adolescence and developed a variety of answers. Some people say that sexual intercourse between engaged couples is all right because they are going to marry anyway. Others say that sexual intercourse between individuals who care for each other is all right, since sex is a way of expressing love. Still others say that sex is simply a biological function and even love and commitment are not necessary. Of course, these answers are not compatible with biblical standards.

Unfortunately, the church has largely ignored this new problem created by the invention of adolescence. Christians continue to say that sexual intercourse before marriage is wrong (and it is), but they do not tell adolescents what to do with their sexuality. The church has accepted our culture's invention of adolescence, but it has not told its adolescents what to do with their sexual desires. As Christian parents you must wrestle with this problem and help your adolescents develop a Christian view of their sexuality.

Sex in Your Sleep

If people are not regularly having sexual intercourse while awake, they are likely to have sexual orgasms in their sleep. These nocturnal emissions, or "wet dreams," are more likely to occur in men than women. In fact, about one man in eight has his first ejaculation this way. Only masturbation is more common than this for a first orgasm.

About 83% of all men have nocturnal emissions and 99% of college men do. It is not college that causes them, but since most of them are single longer while they are in college, their bodies find some sexual outlet. Even though nocturnal emissions occur frequently in the late teens before marriage, they usually decrease or stop completely after marriage.

Nocturnal emissions occurred in Old Testament times, and are dealt with briefly in its early books. Unfortunately, in attempting to find what the Bible says about them, some Christians have taken verses out of context. Nocturnal emissions were clearly referred to only once. "If one of your men is unclean because of a nocturnal emission, he is to go outside the camp and stay there. But as evening approaches he is to wash himself, and at sunset he may return to the camp" (Deut. 23:10-11). Nocturnal emissions were rarely mentioned in the Bible, probably because people were often married at puberty and wet dreams were rare.

The man was referred to as being "unclean" or "defiled" because of his nocturnal emission. Some people have equated this with being sinful, but that is not the case. This referred to being *ceremonially unclean* and not allowed to take part in Jewish religious exercises. A menstruating woman was unclean for a week, and anyone who touched her or even touched something she sat on was unclean that day (Lev. 15:19-23). Note the variety of ways one can become unclean in the following verses and how one becomes clean again: uncleanness does not mean sinfulness.

He will also be unclean if he touches something defiled by a corpse or by anyone who has an emission of semen, or if he touches any crawling thing that makes him unclean, or any person who makes him unclean, whatever the uncleanness may be. The one who touches any such thing will be unclean till evening. He must not eat any of the sacred offerings unless he has bathed himself with water. When the sun goes down, he will be clean, and after that he may eat the sacred offerings, for they are his food. (Lev. 22:4-7)

Everybody Does It!

Someone said, "Ninety-five percent of men admit having masturbated, and the other 5% are liars." Most sexual surveys agree with the 95% figure, but we must not conclude that the others are lying. Some men have less sexual desire, and others are having sexual intercourse regularly. Masturbation is not as common among women, but more than two-thirds of them have masturbated.

Masturbation is the chief type of sexual outlet during early adolescence at every social level. In fact, more than two-thirds of men have their first ejaculation this way, the most common way for them to start having orgasms. At its peak during adolescence, masturbation declines in later adulthood.

Sometimes masturbation is called "just a normal part of growing up." Since we prohibit marriage so long after puberty during the time of greatest sexual desire, it is a part of growing up in our culture. It is not "normal" in the sense that it has always occurred, but adolescents in our society, unable to satisfy their sexual desires with a spouse, often masturbate. Masturbation by so many people is a result of our creation of adolescence.

What does the Bible say? Although secular authors in biblical times wrote about masturbation, the Bible says nothing about it. Even Christians who condemn masturbation today agree that the Bible does not discuss it directly. Of course, the Bible probably does not talk about it because masturbation was apparently much less common back then—when adolescence did not exist and people were having sexual intercourse as married teen-agers.

Unfortunately, people have often misinterpreted three passages in the *King James Version* as talking about masturbation. The first one was when Onan failed to carry out the Levirate marriage law (Deut. 25:5-10). "And Onan knew that the seed should not be his; and it came to pass, when he went in unto his brother's wife, that he spilled it on the ground, lest that he should give seed to his brother. And the thing which he did displeased the Lord: wherefore He slew him also" (Gen. 38:9-10, KJV). Masturbation was sometimes called "Onanism" and condemned as sinful because of this. However, today people agree that Onan practiced coitus interruptus, withdrawing before ejaculating, rather than masturbation.

"Woe to them that devise iniquity, and work evil upon their beds! When the morning is light, they practice it, because it is in the power of their hand" (Micah 2:1, KJV). If you read the context and the verse in a modern translation, you will find that this verse refers to evil in general being planned at night and carried out during the day. People who masturbated with their hands in bed in the morning probably projected what they were doing into the particular wording of the *King James Version*.

Finally, "abusers of themselves with mankind," are listed along with adulterers, thieves, and many others as those who will not "inherit the kingdom of God" (1 Cor. 6:9, KJV). Because of the misinterpretation of this verse, masturbation has been called "self-abuse" and condemned as sinful. Again, if you read this verse in a modern translation, you will find that it is not about masturbation, but about homosexual behavior.

What do Christians say? Since the Bible does not deal with masturbation, people have come to different conclusions about it. A hundred years ago it was condemned by nearly everyone. O.S. Fowler called it "the worst form of excessive and perverted amativeness." John Newman said it was a "crime wholly unnatural and . . . worthy only of brutes like the dog-faced monkey." In 1866 a doctor said that the effects of "this horrible vice are the more pernicious the earlier it is practiced." Masturbation was blamed for causing nearly every disease from acne to insanity.

By the middle of the twentieth century physicians and psychologists found that masturbation caused neither physical nor mental illness. Rather than seeing it as harmful, people began encouraging masturbation. They said that it felt good, released tension, was legal, was always available, was not hazardous to health, and helped one learn to control orgasm.

Modern Christians have taken positions as varied as those held by secular persons. Some believe that masturbation is sinful. For example, widely read Christian author Jay Adams agrees that the Bible makes no direct reference to it, but in *The Christian Counselor's Manual* (Baker) he has a chapter section titled, "Masturbation Is Sin." He believes that the following four general biblical principles apply: We must not be mastered by anything; it is adultery of the heart; it is not presented as a biblical option; and it constitutes a perversion of the sexual act.

Other Christians take the opposite position. For example, in *The Stork Is Dead*, Charlie Shedd (Word) has a chapter titled, "Masturbation—Gift of God." He writes that it can be a positive part of an adolescent's total development. Perhaps past generations were just blind to the truth. Masturbation may simply be the "wise provision of a very wise creator" who "gave it to us because He knew we'd need it" (p. 73) Shedd advises adolescents to thank God for it and to use it as a blessing.

Still other Christians have treated masturbation as a gray area, neither clearly right nor clearly wrong. In his book *Sexual Understanding Before Marriage*, Herbert Miles (Zondervan) has chapter

sections on "When is masturbation sinful?" and "When is masturbation not sinful?" He concludes that though masturbation may be
sinful in some cases, when practiced on a limited, temporary basis
for the purpose of self-control, guided by Christian principles, and
with no evil results, it is acceptable. Obviously Christians do not
agree about the rightness or wrongness of masturbation.

At Least, Everybody Thinks about It!
Perhaps not all adolescents daydream about sex, but almost all do.
In the 1930s psychologists Laurance Shaffer and Edward Shoben
asked nearly 200 college students if they had ever daydreamed
about certain topics and if they had recently done so. Sex was near
the top of the list, and there was little difference between the men
and the women. Among the men, 97% reported having had
sexual daydreams, and 74% reported having had them recently.
Among the women 96% reported having had them, and 73%
having had them recently (*The Psychology of Adjustment* [2nd
ed.], Houghton Mifflin).

Why would almost all adolescents daydream about sex at one
time or another? We imagine things we want but cannot have.
Well-fed people do not daydream about food, but starving people
do—even people on a diet do. Adolescents are not able to have
sex whenever they want it, so they have sexual fantasies. Because
the church says they should not have intercourse, Christian adolescents may have even more sexual fantasies than other adolescents
who are engaging in other sexual activity.

What does the Bible say? Sexual fantasy is certainly nothing
new, but such fantasy by large numbers of single adults is. The
Bible says nothing specific about adolescent sexual fantasy. It could
not, because adolescence did not exist.

While elaborating on the commandment against adultery in the
Sermon on the Mount, Jesus said, "But I tell you that anyone who
looks at a woman lustfully has already committed adultery with her
in his heart" (Matt. 5:28). Notice that He was talking about
adultery, not premarital sex. He was talking about sexual fantasy
by married people, not adolescents. Since people could marry as
soon as they became sexually mature, sexual fantasy before mar-

riage was apparently not as widespread.

What do Christians say? Leading Christians disagree about sexual fantasy. Some say that if Jesus was equating lust with adultery after marriage, lust would likewise be equivalent to pre-marital sex. Some adolescents feel guilty if they have any thoughts about sex. I have known adolescents who struggled with sexual thoughts to the point of asking God to completely take away their sexual desires. A few years later, as their wedding day approached, they were glad that God had not answered their prayers.

Christian author Letha Scanzoni (*Sex Is a Parent Affair,* Regal) says that some sexual fantasies can be good if they are a way of planning for the future, a way of thinking how one would act before the experience occurs. She says that if one concentrates on the beauty of sex in marriage and does not imagine intercourse with an acquaintance, fantasy is acceptable.

Tim and Beverly LaHaye (*The Act of Marriage,* Zondervan) point out that sexual fantasy about your own spouse is not evil. Of course, this is no help to adolescents since they do not have spouses. All the LaHayes can offer single people is to "force your mind" to have only pure (nonsexual?) thoughts about other people. Obviously, Christians disagree about adolescent sexual fantasy.

What Can Parents Do?
The sexual issues are the most difficult problems of adolescence. We must remember that adolescence is a sexual event. By its very definition it begins at puberty, when people become sexually mature. It ends when society treats those people as adults, and one part of that is allowing people to marry and express themselves sexually with a spouse. Adolescent sexual issues are emotionally charged, the Bible is not clear on many of them, and Christians disagree.

Tell them they are normal. Guy, a Christian teenager, was angry with God. He said, "God is really cruel. He gives me these strong sexual drives but won't let me get married. He must like to see people get frustrated." What would you tell Guy? The main thing is to make sure he understands that keeping him from marrying is not God's idea. In fact, before we created adolescence, he could have married.

You must make sure your teenagers realize that there is nothing wrong with them when they have sexual desires. Your adolescents may believe that they are oversexed, that they should not have the sexual desires they have. The problem is with their culture, not with them. Their new sexual desires are right on time, but their culture will not allow them to marry as teens and express those desires in marriage.

This does not mean that you approve of sexual intercourse before marriage. It means only that you accept the fact that strong sexual desires arise long before marriage is possible today. These desires are not sinful, but may lead to temptations that people of other times did not experience. The real problem is what to do with sexual desires, since society does not allow teens to marry.

Prepare them for puberty. Fourteen-year-old Ken woke up at 2:30 in the morning, realizing that something had happened. His pajamas were wet, but sticky—not like he had wet the bed. He thought maybe he was sick and could not urinate because he felt odd, but when he went to the bathroom everything seemed to be all right. He was frightened, but finally got back to sleep.

Sitting with her legs crossed twelve-year-old Clarissa noticed that when she swung one leg, it felt good. One afternoon while doing this, tension built up between her legs and suddenly something happened and she felt all relaxed. Her mother had talked with her about her menstrual periods which would start soon and she thought maybe that was what happened. But that wasn't it, so she was puzzled and a bit frightened. We need to prepare our adolescents for these orgasms. Teenagers who have them unexpectedly may be frightened and think that something is wrong with them.

During the last century some people called nocturnal emissions "vile personal pollutions" and saw them as sexual sin. They tried valiantly to stop these orgasms, but were largely unsuccessful in unmarried men. Some of these old attitudes are still around, and we must see that our teenagers are not troubled by them. We need to tell our teens that wet dreams are a sign of sexual maturity, not sin. They should realize they have so many of them because of the invention of adolescence. If adolescence had not been created, they would probably be married and having regular sexual intercourse with few nocturnal orgasms.

Be available to talk with your teenagers when they are ready. You may feel like talking during the day or early evening, but they may want to talk later. As one father put it, "My teens don't even seem to be able to carry on a conversation before midnight." You will get much further talking with them when they arrive home late at night if they are ready to talk than if you try to wait until morning because you are sleepy. When they wake up, they often have little to say and do not want to listen.

Be sure they understand that people are different. Puberty comes at different ages. It comes as early as nine or ten in some girls, and not until as late as seventeen or eighteen in some boys. Some are tall, but others are short. Some are fat, and others are thin. Some have strong sexual desires, while others are relatively uninterested. Teenagers need to realize that they, like other adults, are varied.

Share your struggles. As I teach adolescents and talk with them, I find that they most often say, "I just wish Dad and Mom would share their own struggles with me." Your teenagers want to know about your struggles with your own sexuality when you were teenagers. You may seem to present an image of a person who had no sexual conflicts as a teenager, and they have a hard time believing it. They want to know that you experienced adolescence and really understand what they are going through.

They also want to know what struggles you are having now. Since the Bible does not say anything about masturbation and Christians disagree, they want to know where you stand on the matter. They want to know if you have reached any conclusions. Your conclusions or current thinking can be of real help to your teenagers. Of course, you must be careful what you say. Sexual orgasms are not evil in themselves. Putting a load of guilt about sex on your teenagers will probably not help at all. If they are already masturbating, the guilt may increase rather than decrease it. God did not condemn masturbation in the Bible, but neither did He encourage it. It has become an expected part of growing up only with the invention of adolescence.

Warn them that fantasy is forever. Remember the rabbi in chapter 1 who said he was superior to his colleagues because he had married at sixteen, and he would have been free of sexual fantasy if he had married at fourteen. Memories are permanent, and adolescent sexual fantasies often reappear later, in marriage. Even when they want to think about their spouses, those old thoughts may return to plague them. Old habits are hard to break, and when problems come in their marriages, people are likely to return to their adolescent fantasies.

Many adolescents turn to pornography while masturbating and to stimulate their fantasy lives. This may lead to wrong conceptions of sex and should be avoided. The people in the pictures in the magazines do not even look like real people because makeup artists work on them before taking the pictures. Adolescents who have fantasized while looking at these pictures may be disappointed in what real people look like.

Sex researcher Shere Hite noted that pornography often shows "women writhing and arching like wild horses during orgasm" (*The Hite Report*, Dell, p. 152). She noted that most women become tense and rigid and lie stiff and still during orgasm. If they move at all, it is a spastic type of movement. Adolescents who fantasize about sex from pornography may be disappointed in the actions of real people. They need to be warned about the misconceptions pornographers are giving them.

Furthermore, pornography loses its appeal. The 1970 Commission on Obscenity and Pornography exposed college men to pornography for an hour and a half a day, five days a week, for three weeks. On the first day the acid phosphatase levels in the urine (an index of sexual arousal) nearly doubled. The second day it was only about a third higher, and it continued to drop as the experiment went on. The first day the men looked at the material 84% of the time. Then each succeeding day they spent less and less time with it. It lost its appeal in a matter of days.

New material results in sexual arousal, as anyone who uses pornography can tell you. That is why magazines such as *Playboy, Playgirl,* and *Penthouse* can successfully publish a new magazine every month. The old ones no longer arouse the people who bought them, so they sell the old ones to used bookstores and buy new ones. Theaters have to schedule new X-rated movies every week because the old ones lose their appeal. Adolescents who use pornography are setting themselves up for needing a new sexual stimulus every few days or weeks, not for a lifetime of marriage to one person.

In an experiment at Arizona State University men and women viewed either nudes from *Playboy, Playgirl,* and *Penthouse* or slides of abstract art. Then they evaluated their own mates. Those who had seen the nudes rated their mates as less attractive sexually, and said they felt less love for them. Sexual fantasy makes real people less desirable. Adolescents should know that.

Distinguish between temptation and sin. Tired of studying, Woody was letting his gaze wander when he noticed how attractive Eloise looked today. Suddenly he realized that he had an erection. He had not meant to do anything wrong, but he felt guilty. Had he lusted and sinned? That afternoon he went to talk with his youth minister.

The minister pointed out that when Jesus talked about lust in the Sermon on the Mount, He was not talking about passing sexual thoughts. That verse might better be translated to say that if you "look at a woman in order to lust after her," you have committed adultery with her. That is, the purpose of your looking is to lust. Furthermore, the word for lust is a very strong word meaning to *desire greatly,* not just noticing that the person is sexually attractive.

Adolescents should not feel guilty for having sexual thoughts or sexual arousal. Most people who understand the difference between temptation and sin can tell when they have crossed the line. Adolescents are adults and will have sexual desires and sexual thoughts. Only they can tell when they get into sexual sin.

You can control much of what comes into your home that would be likely to lead to sexual temptation. Magazines, records, television shows, posters, videos, and so forth are often the source of such temptation. You can keep such things from your home and ask your adolescents to do the same. This itself can help your adolescents control their thought lives.

The Apostle Paul gives good advice when he says, "Finally, brothers, whatever is true, whatever is noble, whatever is right, whatever is pure, whatever is lovely, whatever is admirable—if anything is excellent or praiseworthy—think about such things" (Phil. 4:8). The best way to keep from thinking about wrong things is to think about right things.

The sexual activities discussed in this chapter are all solitary ones. They do not involve other persons. Ideally sexual activity implies commitment and communication in marriage, but our culture makes that illegal, so our adolescents satisfy their sexual desires by themselves. You can help them deal with nocturnal emissions, masturbation, and sexual fantasy.

CHAPTER SEVEN

Should I or Shouldn't I?

Kevin and Kay had dated for three weeks and were going further and further in physically expressing their affection for each other. They had held hands, kissed, and embraced on their first date, but they had gone far beyond that since then. The first week their hands had stayed above the waist. The second week they had gone below the waist, but outside their clothes.

This week their hands were inside each other's clothes, and they found themselves more and more frustrated. They talked about it together. The first week Kevin had said, "Everyone pets." Kay hardly even questioned that. This week Kevin was saying, "Everyone has sex."

Kay found herself wanting it too. She came home from every date sexually aroused, asking herself, "Should I or shouldn't I?"

The question became more difficult when she and Kevin began having orgasms during their petting. Kevin said, "We really care for each other and we aren't being promiscuous."

Kay wondered, "Since we have done 'everything' together, what difference does it make if we have intercourse? Should we or shouldn't we?"

How Far Can We Go?

Kevin and Kay, along with many other adolescents, are wrestling with questions that hardly existed a hundred or more years ago. Premarital sex was still generally considered wrong, but sexual desires were present when adolescence was invented. Dating, a new courtship behavior, was developed. Petting (physical contact intended to cause sexual arousal but not followed by intercourse) became an accepted and expected part of courtship by the 1920s.

There are no standard definitions of petting. Some people try to make distinctions relating to how far the couple goes. They use terms such as necking, light petting, medium petting, and heavy petting, but there is little agreement on what the terms mean. Since petting can include anything except putting the penis into the vagina, some people call heavy petters "technical virgins." That is, they are virgins, but only technically, because they are very experienced sexually. Others call them "promiscuous virgins." The French call them *demi-vierges* (half-virgins).

Since there are no standard definitions of petting, we have little data about the various activities that actually occur. Surveys do show that at least nine out of ten adolescents are involved in some kind of petting, and over half pet to orgasm before they marry. Although more men than women used to be involved in petting, today the percentages are about the same.

Sociologists Ira Robinson and Davor Jedlicka ("Change in Sexual Attitudes and Behavior of College Students from 1965 to 1980: A Research Note, *Journal of Marriage and the Family,* 1982, 44, pp. 237-240) at the University of Georgia did a series of surveys in 1965, 1970, 1975, and 1980. They asked college students whether or not they engaged in light, medium, or heavy petting. Light and medium petting decreased over the years among both men and women, but they did not stop petting. Heavy petting *increased* from 71% in 1965 to 85% in 1980 for men, and from 34% in 1965 to 73% in 1980 for women.

Petting has become generally accepted where strong affection exists. However, it is also becoming more accepted even where there is little affection. In 1959 only 18% of the women and 34% of the men approved if no strong affection existed. By 1972, 30%

of the women and 68% of the men approved (Morton Hunt, *Sexual Behavior in the 1970s*, Dell). That is, people do not have even to really like each other to pet. It is just another activity on a date, like watching a movie or bowling.

Dr. Aaron Hass of the Department of Psychiatry, UCLA School of Medicine, surveyed more than 600 teenagers between the ages of fifteen and eighteen. Among the men 98% believed in was okay for someone their age to touch a woman's breasts, and among the women 91% thought it was okay to let a man touch her breasts. Furthermore, 44% of the men and 18% of the women would want to on the first or second date, and an additional 18% of the men and 24% of the women would want to do so within the first two weeks (*Teenage Sexuality*, Macmillan). That is, about half would begin petting within the first two weeks of their acquaintance.

What does the Bible say? As you might expect, when we turn to find what the Bible says about petting, we find nothing. In Bible times people could marry at puberty, so sexual contact of any kind before marriage was rare. In addition, petting was not a part of courtship. Caressing another person's body was part of marital sex.

Out of fear Isaac had told King Abimelech that Rebekah was his sister instead of his wife. "When Isaac had been there a long time, Abimelech king of the Philistines looked down from a window and saw Isaac caressing his wife Rebekah. So Abimelech summoned Isaac and said, 'She is really your wife! Why did you say, "She is my sister"?' " (Gen. 26:8-9) The *King James Version* says they were "sporting." *The Living Bible* says they were "petting."

Whatever they were doing, Abimelech's response is most interesting. Seeing them fondling each other, he immediately came to the conclusion that they were married. Today, if you looked out the window and saw two people caressing in the bushes, would you think they were married? Probably not.

What do Christians say? Since the Bible does not say anything specific about petting, Christians hold a wide variety of opinions about what is acceptable. These range from no physical contact at all to anything short of intercourse. Some Christian high schools do not permit dating. Their official policy is no physical contact until the students have graduated at eighteen. Other people list things single people can do on dates and include everything up through petting to orgasm.

In *Sexual Understanding Before Marriage* (Zondervan), Herbert Miles noted that adolescents often try to distinguish between holding hands and "relatively unstimulating kissing and embracing" (p. 63). He said that not only is heavy petting unacceptable, but that there is no such thing as unstimulating kissing and embracing. These are sexually stimulating, and usually lead to more sexual activity—to petting and even to intercourse.

In *Sex for Christians* (Eerdmans), Fuller Theological Seminary professor Lewis Smedes has a chapter titled, "Responsible Petting." He says, "Petting can be a delicately tuned means of mutual discovery." It can be a "process in which two people explore each other's feelings." In it "communication can take place that conveys personal closeness and sharing." Petting can be "an adventure in personal understanding and intimacy" (pp. 151-152). Of course, Smedes recognizes that this seldom happens. When adolescents pet, it is not usually at such a sensitive level.

As we found in the last chapter, when the Bible says nothing about those aspects of sexual behavior increased by the invention of adolescence, Christians have widely varying views. Now we will consider actual sexual intercourse by adolescents.

Is It Really That Bad?

Our society has responded to the problem of sexual frustration created by adolescence by saying that there is no need to remain sexually frustrated. Premarital intercourse has become common among both men and women. As one teen put it, "Chastity has no more value than malnutrition." Another said, "Chaste makes waste." Still another said, "Use it or lose it."

Catherine Chilman did an extensive review of studies on adolescent sexuality in the United States for the federal government (*Adolescent Sexuality in a Changing American Society: Social and Psychological Perspectives,* U.S. Department of Health, Education, and Welfare, Publication No. 80-1426). She found that between 1925 and 1965 about 25% of the men and 10% of the women had had intercourse by the time they were seniors in high school. By the end of college about 55% of the men and 25% of the women had had intercourse.

Then came the drastic changes of the late 1960s, and the sexual double standard was nearly erased. By the mid 1970s about 35% of both men and women had had intercourse before they graduated from high school. About 85% of the men and 60-70% of the women did before graduating from college. She concluded that in less than a decade there was a 50% increase among men and a 300% increase among women!

Using a carefully drawn national probability sample, Melvin Zelnik, Young Kim, and John Kantner of the Johns Hopkins University School of Hygiene and Public Health ("Probabilities of Intercourse and Conception Among U.S. Teenage Women, 1971 and 1976, *Family Planning Perspectives,* 1979, *11,* pp. 177-183) found that by 1976 about one unmarried teenager in five became pregnant before she turned nineteen. These adolescents are not becoming pregnant without sexual intercourse.

You may say, "Is it really that bad? Surveys are of what people *say* they do, not of observations of what they *actually* do. Maybe this increase is just more talk, not more sex." Other, more objective evidence also indicates that premarital sexual activity has increased dramatically in recent years.

In 1940 only one child in twenty-nine was born to an unmarried woman. Today one child in every six is born without a legal father. Between 1965 and 1975 alone the illegitimate birth rate increased by more than 50% for teenagers. This was in spite of the fact that contraception became more available and more reliable—and abortion was legalized.

Of course, we must add to those illegitimacy rates the fact that about a third of the births to teenage wives are conceived before marriage, so they are not reported as illegitimate. We really do not know much about the incidence of abortion before 1973. We do know that today for every 100 children born alive to unmarried women there are about 66 abortions. These fetuses are not reported as illegitimate births, so we also have to add them to the illegitimacy rates.

Finally, we must add sexually transmitted diseases. The most common "specified reportable disease" today is not chicken pox or strep throat. It is gonorrhea. With the discovery of penicillin and other antibiotics in the 1940s, many people believed that venereal diseases would be stamped out within a generation or two. That was not the case. Gonorrhea has increased dramatically and is now reported five times as often as chicken pox.

Chlamydia, another venereal disease which is often misdiagnosed and is sometimes symptom-free, may infect five times as many people as gonorrhea. By the 1980s genital herpes had taken the limelight. Since it is not a "specified reportable disease," no one is sure how many people have it. The Center for Disease Control estimates that about 20 million Americans do, and there is no cure for it. These millions of people are not catching such diseases from toilet seats. They are having sexual intercourse.

What does the Bible say? The Bible says remarkably little about premarital sex. We must remember that it was not much of a problem in times when people could marry at puberty. The Bible discusses adultery at length and even prohibits it in the Ten Commandments. If people were having sexual intercourse outside marriage, it was much more likely to be adultery than premarital sex.

Now Joseph was well-built and handsome, and after a while his master's wife took notice of Joseph and said, "Come to bed with me!"

But he refused. "With me in charge," he told her, "my master does not concern himself with anything in the house; everything he owns he has entrusted to my care. No one is greater in this house than I am. My master has withheld nothing from me except you, because you are his wife. How then could I do such a wicked thing and sin against God?" And though she spoke to Joseph day after day, he refused to go to bed with her or even be with her. (Gen. 39:6-10)

Joseph was "a young man of seventeen" (Gen. 37:2) when he dreamed about his brothers bowing down to him. Soon after that he was sold into slavery. Although he was about the ideal age for marriage, he was still unmarried. Notice that he told Potiphar's wife it would be "a wicked thing" and a "sin against God" for him, an unmarried young man, to go to bed with her.

If a young woman was not a virgin when she married, she could be stoned. "She shall be brought to the door of her father's house and there the men of her town shall stone her to death. She has done a disgraceful thing in Israel by being promiscuous while still in her father's house. You must purge the evil from among you" (Deut. 22:21). Thus, it was "disgraceful" or "evil" for a woman to have sexual intercourse before she married.

In the New Testament the words "fornication" or "immorality" are sometimes used to refer to premarital sex. The Greek word is *porneia* and refers to intercourse with prostitutes (especially temple prostitutes) and with a variety of partners. Fornication includes not only premarital sex, but any sexual relationship outside marriage. We must not assume that every time the word occurs it refers to premarital sex, because it refers to adultery as well. But in three passages (Matt. 15:19; Mark 7:21; and 1 Cor. 6:9) it is used with adultery, indicating a difference between the two. Like the Old Testament, the New Testament says relatively little about premarital sex, but enough to indicate that it is wrong.

Best of Friends!

At one time people in our culture generally believed that homosexual behavior was sinful. Then we passed laws against it and made it criminal. Then mental health professionals decided that it was a mental illness. Finally in 1973 the American Psychiatric Association decided that it was not an illness, just an alternative lifestyle.

While people are engaging in premarital sex much more, they are talking about homosexual behavior more. We even have a new, generally accepted, better sounding word for it—"gay." With all the publicity about the gay rights movement, one might think that the number of people with homosexual experiences is increasing. However, that number has remained about the same or even decreased during the last forty years.

Around 1950 Alfred Kinsey and his associates (*Sexual Behavior in the Human Male,* Saunders; and *Sexual Behavior in the Human Female,* Saunders) reported that about 37% of the men and 9% of the women had some homosexual experience by the age of twenty. However, a recent reanalysis of his data showed that he had overestimated the percentage of people involved.

More recent studies have found much lower percentages. In her study for the Department of Health, Education, and Welfare, Catherine Chilman concluded that only about 10% of adolescent men and 5% of adolsecent women have homosexual relations at least once during their teen years.

Whatever the percentages, it does occur, especially during adolescence. If people have a homosexual experience, chances are two out of three that they will have it before they are fifteen years old. Early-maturing men are twice as likely to have homosexual experiences as are late-maturing men, and their frequency remains twice as high.

We must consider the possibility that with our invention of adolescence, we have created a situation that encourages homosexual activity. We take persons at the height of their sexual desire and tell them that they cannot marry. We take two sexually frustrated individuals of the same sex who are not sure of their identity and ask them to share the same dormitory room. We ask individuals of the same sex to take showers together after physical education classes. Then we express surprise, shock, and disgust if they are sexually attracted to each other.

As with premarital sex, the Bible does not dwell at length on homosexual behavior. However, both the Old and New Testaments prohibit it. "Do not lie with a man as one lies with a woman; that is detestable" (Lev. 18:22). "If a man lies with a man as one lies with a woman, both of them have done what is detestable. They must be put to death; their blood will be on their own heads" (Lev. 20:13).

Because of this, God gave them over to shameful lusts. Even their women exchanged natural relations for unnatural ones. In the same way the men also abandoned natural relations with women and were inflamed with lust for one another.

Men committed indecent acts with other men, and received in themselves the due penalty for their perversion. (Rom. 1:26-27)

All in the Family!

Sometimes sexual activity is with other members of the family instead of with unrelated friends. The media have been giving incest more publicity lately, but it is still apparently relatively rare. Psychoanalyst Sigmund Freud at first thought it occurred frequently, then he concluded that the seductions his patients reported had not really occurred but had been imagined. Sex researcher Alfred Kinsey concluded that incest occurred more frequently in the thinking of counselors than in actual fact.

Listening to the media, one would think that incest is usually a matter of an adult male (father, stepfather, or uncle) seducing a female child or adolescent. The fact is that incest occurs much more often between cousins or between brothers and sisters. Sex researchers William Masters and Virginia Johnson ("Incest: The Ultimate Sexual Taboo," *Redbook,* April 1976, pp. 54-58) believe that incest between adolescents is about five times as common as incest between children and adults. Between adolescents it seems to be less damaging, so it is less likely to be reported, even though it is far more common.

Sex researcher Morton Hunt found that intercourse with fathers, mothers, stepfathers, stepmothers, aunts, uncles, and so forth was reported by only 0.5% of the people or less. That is, only one in 200 or less reported sexual experience with an adult relative. However, 3.6% of the women reported sex with their brothers, and 3.8% of the men reported sex with their sisters. Among women 3.2% reported intercourse with a male cousin, and 9.2% of the men reported it with female cousins. Since our culture will not allow normal married sexual relations, some adolescents turn to family members of the same age, other sexually frustrated adolescents.

Although the Bible does not have many passages on incest, the ones in Leviticus 18 and 20 are very specific. They list all of the relatives with whom one should not have sexual relations. "No one is to approach any close relative to have sexual relations. I am the Lord" (Lev. 18:6). "Do not have sexual relations with your sister, either your father's daughter or your mother's daughter, whether she was born in the same home or elsewhere" (Lev. 18:9). "If a man marries his sister, the daughter of either his father or his mother, and they have sexual relations, it is a disgrace. They must be cut off before the eyes of their people. He has dishonored his sister and will be held responsible" (Lev. 20:17).

A well-known case of incest (and rape) in the Bible occurred in the family of King David. Amnon tricked his sister Tamar into being alone with him, then "he grabbed her and said, 'Come to bed with me, my sister.'

" 'Don't, my brother!' she said to him. 'Don't force me. Such a thing should not be done in Israel! Don't do this wicked thing" (2 Sam. 13:11-12). He would not listen to her. Later, their brother Absalom had him killed for what he had done.

What Can Parents Do?
As you read the percentage of teens involved in sexual activity before marriage, you may say, "Is there any hope? Can we do anything to see that our teenagers are in the 20% that wait until marriage?" Yes, there is hope. Furthermore, you are probably already doing what is most likely to help your teens remain virgins.

In his article "Premarital Sexual Behavior and Religious Adolescents" Timothy Woodroof (*Journal for the Scientific Study of Religion,* 1985, *24,* pp. 343-366) pointed out that during the last forty years every study (with one exception) has found that the more religious adolescents are, the less likely they are to have premarital sex. He concluded that religion was one of the most consistent and powerful influences on adolescent sexual behavior. Even such a simple thing as church attendance was related—the more often teenagers attended church, the less likely they were to be sexually active.

Not only should you encourage your teens to attend church, but you should also encourage them to "internalize" their religion. They need to make a personal commitment to Christ. This is no guarantee that your teen will remain chaste, but it is a giant step in the right direction. Now let us consider some specific steps you can take regarding the topics discussed in this chapter.

What about petting? You should talk about petting with your adolescents before they begin to date. When they start dating, they are likely to begin expressing their feelings physically. Wanting to express those feelings in marriage is normal. However, our culture has invented dating in place of marriage for teenagers. Earlier in the chapter we saw that about half the teens wanted to start petting within the first two weeks. If you wait until after the first date, you may have waited too long.

Jay said, "I can't get married, and I don't believe sex before marriage is right, so I figure petting is the best way to get rid of my frustrations." The truth is exactly the opposite. When petting takes place by married couples, it is called "foreplay." Caressing another person's body is a natural prelude to sexual intercourse. In her review for the Department of Health, Education, and Welfare, Catherine Chilman found that people who pet but do not go on to intercourse are more restless and dissatisfied with their sex lives than are those who do not pet or those who have premarital intercourse. Since petting "naturally" leads to intercourse, petting alone only increases sexual frustration.

Help your adolescents reach some conclusions for themselves about what is acceptable and what is not. These decisions must be made before they find themselves in a sexually aroused state where they cannot think clearly. We simply talked with our teens about what they considered appropriate one step at a time. "Is it all right to hold hands?" "Is it all right to put your arm around the other person's neck or shoulders?" "How about around the other person's waist?" "How about touching a woman's breasts?" and so on until we reached the limit.

A friend of ours had each of her daughters actually write down the parts of their bodies they would allow their dates to touch. Of course, she followed this with a discussion of what she believed was appropriate and *why* she believed what she did. Remember that there is seldom any backing up. Once a couple takes a step, they are very likely to go at least that far on the next date.

One young woman said to me, "Petting can ruin a good

relationship." She was right. Help your teens learn a variety of ways to showing affection—they will need them after they marry. Such things as a small gift or an unexpected note to the other person makes them feel special. A wink or a smile across the room may convey more affection than physical contact. Help them to realize that "everybody does it" is not a good argument.

What about premarital sex? Since the Bible does speak to the issue of premarital sex, you should take a stand on it. When talking with your adolescents, be scriptural about why they should avoid premarital sex. Too often parents give cultural reasons, such as pregnancy or disease, for avoiding sex before marriage. The Bible never mentions these.

Where it mentions sex outside marriage, the Bible talks about being holy. Leviticus 18–20 has extended passages on sexual sins, and in the middle of these are the following. "Speak to the entire assembly of Israel and say to them: 'Be holy because I, the Lord your God, am holy' " (Lev. 19:2). "Consecrate yourselves and be holy, because I am the Lord your God. Keep My decrees and follow them. I am the Lord, who makes you holy" (Lev. 20:7-8). In the New Testament, Paul says, "It is God's will that you should be holy; that you should avoid sexual immorality; that each of you should learn to control his own body in a way that is holy and honorable" (1 Thes. 4:3-4).

Be sure that you and your adolescents agree that premarital sex is wrong. You cannot assume that they think so. A Gallup poll on May 18, 1975 showed that fewer than one out of five college students believed that it was "wrong for people to have sexual relations before marriage." That percentage has remained relatively constant during the last ten years. Today about 80% of teenagers still think there is nothing wrong with sexual relations before marriage.

Gallup polls show that even parents are changing their positions on this. On September 14, 1969, 68% of the general public thought it was wrong. Less than four years later on August 2, 1973, only 48% thought it was wrong. A Roper poll reported in *U.S. News & World Report* (December 9, 1985) showed that the figure had dropped to 36% in the population as a whole. In fact, only

25% of people between 30 and 44 years of age thought it was wrong, and they are often parents of teens. When parents do not believe that it is wrong, teens are more likely to do it.

Encourage your teens to avoid situations leading to temptation. Ask them where they are going on their dates. An unplanned date may lead to intercourse if the couple cannot think of something else to do. Double dating, with the right other couple, can keep physical intimacy at a minimum. Insist that they leave the doors to their rooms open when they are there. Intercourse sometimes takes place while the couple is listening to records in the bedroom, and the parents are in the living room watching television.

Be careful whom your teens date. A 1984 survey of students at the University of South Dakota showed that 48% of the women had been held, kissed, or fondled against their will on dates. In fact, 20.6% said they had experienced "date rape"—they had been physically forced by a dating partner to have sexual intercourse. Tell your daughters that if they find themselves in such a situation, they should reach a phone if at all possible and you will pick them up immediately—any time, anywhere.

One other thing you can do is be at home when your adolescents are there. In their national sample, Zelnik and Kantner ("Sexual and Contraceptive Experience of Young Unmarried Women in the United States, 1976 and 1971," *Family Planning Perspectives*, 1977, *9*, pp. 55–71) asked teenage girls where they had sexual intercourse. Parents typically think sex is taking place in a car, but that only accounted for 6.1% of the times. Motels and hotels accounted for another 6.4%.

Nearly 75% of the sexual activity occurred at home. Twenty-three percent of it was in her home, and 51.2% was in his. As our culture has changed from a home with both parents home most of the time, to a home with the father gone at work but the mother home, to a home with both parents gone at work, the home has become the best place for an adolescent couple to be alone. If no one else is at home, adolescents should not be there alone. We always told our own adolescents that if they came home with their date and no one was there, they should not go in the house alone. This did not mean that we did not trust them, just that we recognized the strength of the temptation.

Probably the most difficult situation for any parent is the need to talk with an adolescent they know is sexually involved. Parents often feel angry and feel like rejecting such a teenager. After all, that "ungrateful kid" is bringing shame on the family. Parents should make every effort to reach these adolescents. Sexual sin can be forgiven just like any other sin.

While you must love and accept that teen, make it clear that you do not accept his or her behavior. Insist on no sexual intercourse at home. If you find contraceptives, do not insist that they be destroyed. You can destroy the birth control and make teens promise to stop having sex, but they will probably not stop. Your next problem will most likely be what to do about an unplanned pregnancy.

What about homosexuality? As parents, see that your adolescents realize that homosexual behavior is wrong, but do not overreact. Some people have developed "homophobia," fear of homosexuality. The Bible deals with homosexual behavior as it does with fornication. It is wrong and we should not do it. Unfortunately, many Christian parents do not try to help their adolescents, but reject them. These adolescents are caught in a sin less socially acceptable than pride, gossip, or even premarital sex, but they need help rather than rejection.

Very hesitantly and with much embarrassment one college man said, "Three times I had an erection in the locker room after my P.E. class. I was so ashamed that I didn't even take a shower. I think I'm 'queer.'" I was able to assure him that adolescent men often have spontaneous erections, and if they have them when other men are around, they may wrongly define themselves as "gay." Becoming sexually aroused in a locker room where naked persons of the same sex are present does not mean the adolescent is a "queer." The temptations toward premarital sex, adultery, or homosexual behavior are all temptations to misuse one's sexuality.

Help your teens avoid situations where temptation may arise. For example, when friends stay overnight, rather than have them sleep in a bed together, put separate sleeping bags on the floor. Talk with them about what to do if they are propositioned at school or in a public rest room.

With all this, do not make them fear same-sex friendships. There is nothing wrong with having friends. What is wrong is becoming sexually involved with them. Finally, talk with them about what to do if they find out that one of their friends is homosexual. When doing this, emphasize that homosexual behavior, like other sinful behavior, can be forgiven.

What about incest? As parents, make it clear to your adolescents that incest is wrong. Again, do not assume that they believe it is wrong. In *Adolescent Sexuality in Contemporary America,* Robert Sorenson (World) reported that 18% of teenagers between thirteen to nineteen years of age did not think it was unnatural for a brother and sister to have sexual relations if both of them wanted to. In addition, 25% of the men and 13% of the women thought sex between parent and child was acceptable.

One specific thing you can do to help prevent it is to have separate rooms for brothers and sisters. Although children of the opposite sex may share a room, adolescents should not. Sexual temptations arise and incest may result. On vacations and trips, teenage brothers and sisters should not share beds, even if parents are in the same motel room.

You need to avoid family nakedness. Sexual temptation can arise when members of the family are unclothed or partially clothed. Teenagers are adults and should be aware that they can become sexually aroused by members of their own family. Modesty at home should be the rule.

Finally, talk with your teens about expressing affection appropriately with relatives. This is not to say that they should be distant from relatives, but that if a relative makes improper advances, teens should respond with a firm no to further contact.

Although the percentage of people involved in sexual sin is alarmingly high and seems to be increasing, your teens can be among the minority who are not involved. They need your support as they live through an adolescence where even more of their friends are sexually active than was the case when you were growing up.

CHAPTER EIGHT

We're Getting Married!

Ed and Ruth were watching the end of the evening movie on television when Ann came in with her boyfriend. Ann had dated Brad all during their junior year in high school and still liked him as they were starting their senior year. Ann was especially bubbly as they sat in the living room talking. She suddenly said, "Mom and Dad, we're getting married!"

Ed and Ruth sat in stunned silence. Finally, Ruth said, "But you're both so young! You're only seventeen and have high school to finish. Then there's college, and maybe even graduate school."

Ann protested, "We're mature enough to have planned for all that. We both have part-time jobs after school, so we can stay in school. Brad is hoping for a basketball scholarship, and I should get an honors one. With the help we get from government grants and loans, we can make it without any problems."

After a rather heated half-hour discussion, Ed concluded with, "You two just don't know what it's all about. It'll never work. We won't give our permission, and you can't marry without it."

Ann ended the conversation by saying, "In four months we'll

both be eighteen and you can't stop us then. We're getting married!"

It'll Never Work!

Such an announcement strikes fear into the hearts of most parents. They have read the statistics: more than half of all teenage marriages end in divorce. Indeed, those marriages do end in divorce, but it is not just because of age. They have many other things against them from the beginning.

Those who marry as teenagers are the least likely persons to make a marriage succeed. They are often people who cannot wait to get what they want. They are also ones who do not conform to society and who expect too much from marriage. Many of the brides are pregnant, so the couple has to adjust not only to marriage, but also to parenthood. Some of them marry to get away from bad home situations only to wind up in worse ones. In general, if you were to try to find people who were least likely to make a success of their marriage, they would be the typical people who marry as teenagers.

After they marry, society makes it difficult for them to live. As we will see in a later chapter, money is usually a problem in teen marriages. If they are still in school, they have little money. When they want to work, they have difficulty finding jobs. When they are hired, it is most likely for temporary jobs with low pay. If you were to design an economic situation to make marriage difficult, you would make it like ours for teens.

In addition, just about everyone tells them that their marriage will fail. Parents and friends quote the latest rate of failure for teen marriages. We already saw the powerful effects of the self-fulfilling prophecy in which people act the way others expect them to. Then when the divorce comes, parents may not say it aloud, but they usually think, "I told you so." The problem is not age as much as it is other factors.

Many people also believe other "facts" that are not necessarily true. Parents believe that children will soon come along. Of course, that is true if the bride is already pregnant, as so many are. However, it is not necessarily true if she is not. In fact, married teenagers may be more likely to use birth control than unmarried ones.

In their national probability sample of teenaged women, Melvin Zelnik and John Kantner ("Reasons for Nonuse of Contraception by Sexually Active Women Aged 15–19," *Family Planning Perspectives,* 1979, *11,* pp. 289–296) found that 65.8% of the pregnant unmarried women did not want their pregnancy. Among these, 85.5% did not use birth control when they became pregnant. They said they did not use it because they did not expect to have intercourse, circumstances prevented it, their partner objected, they thought it was wrong or dangerous, or they thought that sex was not as much fun with birth control.

Unmarried teens may also not use contraceptives because they think it means that their love is not "spontaneous." That does not seem to bother married people. Also, some unmarried teens do not use it because taking such precautions implies that they are planning to be immoral, and they would rather think of themselves as being caught in the pressures of the moment.

Parents of married teens read the statistics on the birth defects and poor health of children born to teenagers. We must consider the fact that many of these children are born to unmarried mothers, who frequently get little prenatal care and live in poor conditions. Both of these can lead to problems in infants.

What would happen to the marriages of older people if they were the same kind of people who marry as teens? What if all marriages started out under conditions of near poverty? What if at every wedding parents and friends told the bride and groom that their marriage probably would not work? Couples at any age would have difficulty making a marriage work under these circumstances .

Radical Celibacy

Although teen marriages worked for thousands of years, we now have a system of celibacy for everyone under eighteen. *Celibacy* literally means "a single life." The dictionary defines a celibate as an unmarried person, especially one who has taken a vow not to marry. Protestants are sometimes critical of the Roman Catholic ideal of celibacy for the clergy, but they raise no voice against something even more radical—celibacy for a whole class of people during the time when some have their greatest sexual desire.

Of course, there is nothing wrong with celibacy. The Bible is clear that celibacy is good. The Apostle Paul said, "It is good for a man not to marry" (1 Cor. 7:1). He went on to say, "Now to the unmarried and the widows I say: It is good for them to stay unmarried, as I am" (1 Cor. 7:8). In the times Paul was living he could say, "He who marries the virgin does right, but he who does not marry her does even better" (1 Cor. 7:38). Jesus Himself is another example, for He lived His entire thirty-three years without marrying.

Certainly celibacy is not wrong, but in our creation of adolescence we have something even more radical. Celibacy, according to its definition, often involves a vow by the celibate person. We do not even give adolescents that choice. We tell them that for the first six or eight years of their adult lives, they cannot legally marry. Furthermore, we seem to believe that we will get chastity if we enforce celibacy.

Chastity means "purity." The dictionary defines *chastity* as refraining from all unlawful sexual activity. Unfortunately, our laws have produced celibacy without chastity. Our adolescents are unmarried, but as we saw in the last chapter, most of them are not abstaining from sexual activity.

The Bible is also clear that celibacy is not for everyone. The passages on celibacy are followed by a clause beginning with "but." Consider the first two passages quoted above. "But since there is so much immorality, each man should have his own wife, and each woman her own husband" (1 Cor. 7:2). "But if they cannot control themselves, they should marry, for it is better to marry than to burn with passion" (1 Cor. 7:9). Paul is clear about his solution to the problem of premarital sex. It is marriage.

When His disciples made their statement about not marrying, Jesus replied, "Not everyone can accept this teaching but only those to whom it has been given. For some are eunuchs because they were born that way; others were made that way by men; and others have renounced marriage because of the kingdom of heaven. The one who can accept this should accept it" (Matt. 19:11-12). This is not an easy passage to understand, but it appears that Jesus saw celibacy as good, but as a special gift. Not everyone should be celibate.

Cultures like ours were anticipated by Paul. "They forbid people to marry and order them to abstain from certain foods, which God created to be received with thanksgiving by those who believe and who know the truth" (1 Tim. 4:3). He was very specific about encouraging younger widows to marry, as he emphasized in the next chapter.

> Give proper recognition to those widows who are really in need. . . . No widow may be put on the list of widows unless she is over sixty, has been faithful to her husband. . . . As for younger widows, do not put them on such a list. For when their sensual desires overcome their dedication to Christ, they want to marry. . . . So I counsel younger widows to marry, to have children, to manage their homes and to give the enemy no opportunity for slander. (1 Tim. 5:3, 9, 11, 14)

Some people today argue that chastity prepares people for "more emphatic experiences of sexual release." This may be true when talking about a matter of hours or days, but it hardly applies to the years of adolescence. This same line of reasoning would say that we should starve adolescents so they would enjoy their food more when they got it or that we should cut off their air so they would appreciate odors more.

Anyone knows that when too hungry, people simply wolf down their food, not even enjoying the delicate tastes. People who have nearly suffocated do not notice the subtle odors in the air they breathe, they are simply interested in gulping as much air as possible. Similarly, there is no evidence that years of adolescent chastity makes sex any more enjoyable later in life.

Not allowing newly matured adults to be sexually active is, in principle, like passing a law against allowing children to walk until they are eight years old. We could tell them that they were not old enough to walk. If they wanted to walk, they would have to walk secretly. We can only imagine the effect of that on their walking when they became adults. Likewise, we can only speculate about the effect of not allowing normal sexual expression during the first six to eight years of a person's adult life.

The problem is not that sexual feelings occur too early in our culture, but that because of adolescence, weddings occur too late. The biblical answer to the sexual problems of teenagers was to not have adolescence. The church has accepted our culture's invention of adolescence, but it has not told its adolescents what to do with their sexual desires.

They Don't Know What It's All About!

As parents you may look at your teenagers and say that someone that age with so little experience cannot know what marriage is all about. You think, "Having an adolescent picking a marriage partner is like having someone who has never driven buy a car." You are right! Such a person may buy a car that is pretty and rides well, without considering how long the car will last or how well it will run under difficult conditions. You have lived in a marriage relationship and believe, quite correctly, that you know more about picking a marriage partner than do your adolescents who have no experience as spouses.

Of course "courtship" used to be quite different from what it is now. For example, when Abraham decided it was time for Isaac to marry, he called his chief servant and said, "I want you to swear by the Lord, the God of heaven and the God of earth, that you will not get a wife for my son from the daughters of the Canaanites, among whom I am living, but will go to my country and my own relatives and get a wife for my son Isaac" (Gen. 24:3-4).

The servant agreed and went to find Isaac a wife. When he had found the woman and explained his mission, her father said, "Here is Rebekah; take her and go, and let her become the wife of your master's son, as the Lord has directed" (Gen. 24:51). Isaac and Rebekah were not "in love," but they had many other things more important in a marriage. (The "love" came later. Remember that it was Isaac and Rebekah who were caressing, or sporting, or petting, when Abimelech looked out his window.)

As we read this account, we find that they came from good families where their parents served God. She was beautiful, a virgin, industrious, and hospitable (vv. 16, 19, 25). When the servant set out to convince her parents that she should marry Isaac, he talked about God's blessing and Abraham's (Isaac's father) material wealth (v. 35). We might think that Rebekah would be hesitant to marry a stranger whom she had never met, but that was not the case. When Abraham's servant wanted to leave right away, her mother wanted her to stay another ten days.

"Then they said, 'Let's call the girl and ask her about it.' So they called Rebekah and asked her, 'Will you go with this man?'

" 'I will go,' she said" (Gen. 24:57-58). Then they left immediately.

All of this seems very businesslike to us who emphasize romantic love. The marriage brokers of the Romans looked at such things, and we need to as well. We often forget that marriage is a legal contract, one more binding than any other in our society. People cannot legally enter this contract without permission from the state—a license. They cannot enter the contract unless it is approved by another person—the minister or justice of the peace. The contract must be observed by two others—the witnesses. When they enter this contract, each becomes responsible for nearly everything the other person does—such as buying on credit. They cannot break the contract without permission from the state—a judge. And sometimes there are legal obligations even after the contract is broken—alimony and child support.

Today we use the "trapping model" of courtship. I used to run a trap line and I see many of the same techniques used in trying to catch a mate. First, the trap must be in the right place. Some people set it in a singles bar, others in a church. Second, the trap must be hidden. People try not to be too transparent with the one they are trying to catch. Third, the set must look just right. Hair sprays, makeup, clothes, and shoes are sold to make teens look "irresistible" to the ones they are trying to catch. Finally, the bait must smell right. Deodorants, mouthwashes, soaps, breath mints, perfumes, and colognes are the final touches to make teenagers smell right.

Parents used to match people who would be good spouses, and they would grow to love each other. Today adolescents pick someone they "love," then try to make them into good mates. Unfortunately, you cannot love someone you do not really know. You do not really get to know a person until you have lived with them for some time, and marriage in our society is often not strong enough to keep people together for that love to grow. Of course, the meaning of "love" has changed. When adolescents say they love each other, they usually mean they find each other attractive, not that they want to give themselves for each other.

Unfortunately, we often take more care in picking a business partner or a vocation than we do in picking a spouse. We may carefully investigate a business partner, but we pick a spouse on the basis of romantic love, then enter a legal contract with them. Yet the two major problems in most marriages are sex and money. We pick a mate who is sexually attractive, and then find that we are not sexually satisfied. Looking at how they handle money seems too businesslike to be considered in courtship; then we are unhappy when their values are different from ours.

Teenagers today need to be even more careful in choosing a mate than people were in the past. People live much longer today than they did even a century ago, which means that marriages last longer. When people died at an average of forty or fifty years of age, it meant that most people did not live together nearly as long as they do now. Most people did not live together long after the children left home. Today marriages often last forty or fifty years.

Living Together

One thing that our society has developed to try to improve mate selection is living together for a trial period before marriage. More than a million and a half couples were doing this in 1980. They believed that this would ensure that they would marry only people they knew they could adjust to. They also believed their marriages would be happier because the problems that usually come up early in marriage would have already been worked out. They would have decided on how to share the household chores, the frequency of sexual activity, how to make decisions, and so forth.

Although all of this sounds reasonable, it simply does not work. Many studies have been done comparing such couples with others who have not lived together before marriage, and most have found no differences in their marriages. Their satisfaction with marriage is about the same, and the divorce rates are about the same.

Sociologists Alfred DeMaris of Auburn University and Gerald Leslie ("Cohabitation with the Future Spouse: Its Influence upon Marital Satisfaction and Communication," *Journal of Marriage and the Family,* 1984, *46,* pp. 77-84) of the University of Florida believed that if they did a good enough study they could show that living together before marriage led to a better marriage. They picked their couples very carefully so that they were mostly not college students and all had been married from one to two years. They used a test of marital satisfaction that was more sensitive than others had used.

After analyzing the data from nearly 300 couples, they found the opposite of what they had expected. Both husbands and wives had *lower* marital satisfaction if they had lived with each other before they married than if they did not. Even after controlling for "sex-role traditionalism," church attendance, and everything else they could think of, they found that those who lived together before marriage showed less satisfaction. DeMaris and Leslie finally concluded that people who are willing to live together before marriage do not make good marriage partners.

What Can Parents Do?

As we have seen, teen marriage was not a problem in Bible times. People accepted it and saw marriage itself as a solution to the problem of premarital sex. This is reversed today. Most people in our culture frown on early marriage and consider premarital sex acceptable.

Of course, adolescence is far more than simply forbidding marriage of people under eighteen. As we have seen, our culture has removed identity from teenagers. As we will see in later chapters, our culture discriminates against adolescents so that they cannot support themselves. It also requires them to spend many years in school.

We seem to assume that the way we do things now is an advance over the past, but the bulk of the evidence indicates that we are doing far worse than people did in the past. We should ask ourselves whether *our* system of courtship and marriage works. It clearly does not. When we look at the divorce rates, we see that as we have adopted our modern customs, the long-term success of marriage has declined. Let us consider some things parents can do to help their offspring's marriages succeed.

Treat each one individually. We have been told so often that teenage marriages are bad that we hardly believe they can succeed. If we look for recent sociological or psychological studies that teenage marriages are good, we are not likely to find many. Our culture has stacked the cards against their success. But we have the evidence from thousands of years that early marriages can work. We should not automatically reject the idea of teenage marriage, but consider each case individually.

This means not that we should encourage teen marriage but that it is not necessarily bad. Many teenagers are not socially mature enough for marriage. We have expected them to act like children, and they do. If we had expected them to act like adults, many of them would be mature enough to marry, just as people were in the past. If most teenagers are not socially mature enough for marriage today, it is not their fault, but ours.

Some parents face the very difficult problem of their adolescent dating someone they strongly believe is the wrong person. Marriage is the most important choice people make at the human level. If they choose the wrong college, they can transfer. If they choose the wrong job, they can quit. Although our culture would have us think it is the same with marriage, it is not that simple.

The law gives you power over your adolescents, but you have to earn their respect. Respect is based on competence, wisdom, and experience. It is the "honor" referred to in the fifth commandment: "Honor your father and your mother" (Ex. 20:12). Power, on the other hand, is based on force. Respect requests, but power demands. People I respect have more influence on my life than those who have only power.

If you believe that your adolescent should not marry, use the respect you have earned rather than the power the law gives you. You have the *power* to tell your seventeen-year-old he or she cannot marry, but it will be better if you can delay the marriage using the *respect* your son or daughter has for you. If you command, they may wait only until they reach the age limit, then marry.

If you are divorced, you may have a particular problem in this area. The teenager may think that you have messed up your own life and have nothing to tell them about love and marriage. If this is the case, you may have to call on power or convince your teenager that she or he can learn from your mistakes.

Teach them what it's all about. You were right when you said that they do not know what marriage is all about, but it is up to you to teach them. This means education for marriage in its broadest sense. It includes sex education as well as how to get along as a spouse. In this section we will consider sex education, and we'll discuss getting along in a later chapter.

At this point, you may be thinking, "My adolescents have no trouble talking about sex, I'm the one! I can hardly bring up sexual topics, and when they do come up, I get all tongue-tied."

Perhaps you were raised in a home where sexual activity of any kind was not discussed. You did not talk about it as a child or adolescent, so you find it difficult to discuss it as an adult. Not only do you find it hard to talk about with your own children and adolescents, but with other parents as well. The last two chapters may have been difficult to read. You may even find it hard to discuss sexual matters with your spouse.

You should work toward becoming comfortable discussing sexual matters. If you feel uncomfortable about it, the first thing to do is to determine why. If the problem is that you are unsure of your sexual knowledge, get some books on human sexuality and study them. Since many colleges now offer courses on human sexuality, many good books are available. Taking a course in it may help you too.

If the problem is that you feel guilty, ashamed, or sinful when you talk about sex, you need to do two things. One is to learn and become convinced that sex is not shameful or sinful. In the past when Christians talked about sex, they seemed to major on sex as sin rather than on the positive things about it. You can counter this by studying the positive things the Bible has to say about sex. Reading the positive books mentioned in chapter 6 will also help.

Of course, changing your thinking will not automatically change your feelings of shame or guilt. These are learned responses, so the second thing you need to do is to unlearn them. The only way to get rid of these is to openly discuss sexual topics. Discussion with your spouse will help. Discussion with other parents who feel the same way will help. This can be done in a class on human sexuality at a college or in church. By the end of an evening, you may feel more comfortable, but later the old feelings will come back. You need to have such discussions several times, until the old feelings of shame and guilt are gone. Discussions about sex will probably never become casual, but they need not produce shame and guilt.

You may wonder when to start educating your children about sex. A copy of *Playboy* was confiscated in the first grade of our local elementary school. If you waited until your children were in school, you waited too long. Sexuality education series begin with books for preschool children and follow that with several others for older ages. Get a book appropriate for your children or teens and begin immediately.

Another problem is how to bring sexual topics up for discussion. If you are open with your children and adolescents, such questions will arise naturally. One of our children came home from third grade asking what a four-letter word written on the rest-room wall meant. It was the perfect opening to discuss sexual intercourse more fully and give a wholesome perspective on it.

If you read the Bible in your family devotions, sexual questions will arise, especially if you read a modern translation. Sexual material is not always as concentrated as in Leviticus 18–20, but the New Testament as well as the Old Testament does not ignore human sexuality. Reading Christian sexuality education books with (not just giving them to) your children and adolescents will open many topics. For example, the Concordia series has books for children and adolescents of various ages as well as for parents.

As parents in modern Western society you are not responsible for picking mates for your teenagers, but you are responsible for teaching them how to pick mates and how to be mates. Often adolescents seem to look only at whether or not the person is attractive (the trapping model). They may concentrate on whether the person looks and acts sexy. Does the person "turn them on"? Unfortunately, they may not even look at what the person will be like to live with. They may not consider the person's family or how he or she manages money. They may not watch to see how the person responds when everything seems to go wrong.

Steve came home from a backpacking trip with the church youth group and said, "I think every guy interested in a girl should go backpacking with her." He had been interested in Judy, but on the trip she had complained about everything. Steve did not mind legitimate complaints, but she complained about everything from the weather to the walking—things no one could do anything about. He now knew he would never want to live with her.

Help them make it work. If your teenagers who are of legal age are going to marry against your better judgment, support it. Your continued opposition will only make their marriage more difficult, less likely to succeed. Make sure that both of them understand that they are making a lifetime commitment. Expect the best, remembering how important your expectations are.

If they have not known each other very long, encourage a long engagement. Get both sets of parents together and make sure the adolescents see any differences in the value systems of the two families. Help them realize that a marriage is between two families, as well as between two individuals.

Encourage them to get premarital counseling from a trusted minister. See if they will attend an "engaged discovery" weekend at church where they will be with others who are intending to marry. They can compare themselves with others there and may take what is said there more seriously than what you say.

Remember that teen marriages are not doomed. They worked for thousands of years and many still work today. If your teens are over eighteen, they can marry without your approval. Even if they are under eighteen, if they are mature and both sets of parents support it, the marriage has a good chance of success.

CHAPTER NINE

Why Can't I Work?

Arnold was sitting at his desk, trying to keep his mind on accounting, but having little success. He was tired of studying for exams, and he kept daydreaming about having money to do whatever he wanted. It seemed he never had enough. He imagined himself winning a sweepstakes and having money to buy a car, a boat, a house—and still have lots left over.

Across the campus Penny was lying on her bed, trying to learn physiology. She too had trouble keeping her mind on her studies. She imagined what it would be like when she was a surgeon. She thought about herself examining patients, operating on them, and presenting the findings of her research to other doctors.

What do adolescents daydream about most? We already mentioned that 96% or 97% reported daydreaming about sex. Only two other topics ranked higher in the percentage of students reporting daydreams. In that same study 100% of the college men reported daydreaming about "vocational success" and 100% about "money or possessions." Among college women, 98% daydreamed about vocational success and 97% about money or possessions. (Laurance Shaffer and Edward Shoben, *The Psychol-*

ogy of Adjustment, Houghton Mifflin). Work, money, and sex were the top three.

Why do adolescents daydream about work and money? For the same reason they daydream about sex. They cannot have it.

Although we say we want independence for everyone, we keep adolescents economically dependent. We do not allow them to work, so they do not have their own money. Money gives us power over our adolescents, and many teenagers do not like being kept in this state of dependence. It was not this way until the invention of adolescence a century ago.

Before Adolescence

For thousands of years children worked with and learned a trade from their parents. It seemed only natural that parents should teach their children about work or apprentice them to someone who could teach a different trade. Children worked with their parents in field or factory. They worked beside a master as an apprentice for several years until they could produce their own *masterpiece* and become independent.

During the seventeenth century in the United States, Puritan boys worked, and at about fourteen their fathers chose callings for them. In the eighteenth century Benjamin Franklin wrote that he was taken from school at ten years of age to help in the family business. When he was twelve, his father signed the indenture for him to serve as an apprentice until he was twenty-one.

In the nineteenth century Massachusetts required that no state money be used "for the support of any male person, over the age of twelve, and under the age of sixty years, while of competent health to labor" (*Laws of the Commonwealth of Massachusetts,* 1823). People over twelve were expected to support themselves. In 1900, nearly two-thirds of the men between fourteen and nineteen years old were working. By 1940, only about a third were. What brought about this dramatic change?

It's the Law!

In the nineteenth century a constant labor shortage resulted in children being employed everywhere. In fact, in 1834, 40% of the factory workers in New England were children. In 1842, two states passed laws limiting the hours children could work. Soon a half dozen states prohibited children under ten or twelve from working in factories.

Child labor continued to increase until about 1900. People who cared about children, people who wanted to keep wages up, and people who wanted more efficient labor persuaded legislators to pass the child labor laws. However, rather than just making forced labor illegal, legislators made *all* labor illegal for children. People could begin to work at about the age of puberty. That is, when the laws were passed, they distinguished children from adults. Children could not work, but adults could.

Unfortunately, as the age of puberty decreased, the minimum legal age for work increased. Currently all but five states require special permission to work under a given age. That age is eighteen in twenty-four states, seventeen in three states, sixteen in seventeen states, and fifteen in one state. We now have a situation in which some adults (adolescents), not just children, are prevented from working.

We often hear about the terrible effects of unemployment on people. We are told that it damages the human spirit, that it leads to depression, and that it leads to low self-esteem. Laws meant to protect children now force unemployment on these new adults (adolescents). As the National Commission on Youth (*The Transition of Youth to Adulthood: A Bridge Too Long,* Westview Press, p. 14) put it, "Youth are now isolated, restrained, and eventually victimized by the very institutions designed for their protection."

Yet another set of laws also helps keep many adolescents from working. In 1930 Congress passed a federal minimum wage law covering about five out of ten workers and setting the wage at $0.25 an hour. Today it covers more than nine out of ten workers and is $3.35 an hour.

Although legislators intended these laws to protect workers, their effect was to price adolescents out of the labor market. Employers found it cheaper to automate or to manufacture things in other countries where people would work for less. The National Commission on Youth recommended paying lower wages to youth getting training and experience in apprenticeship and internship programs. If adolescents produce less than other adults, they should be paid less.

Don't Call Us, We'll Call You

When teenagers look for work, they often hear, "Don't call us, we'll call you." Adolescents have great difficulty finding permanent work. In addition to the ways discussed above, several other things have happened in our culture to make unemployment a way of life for them.

For thousands of years people were paid for what they did. Cobblers were paid for each pair of shoes. Blacksmiths were paid for each horse shod. Farmers were paid for the produce they brought to market. People who produced more were paid more. On October 28, 1779, George Washington wrote about visiting a factory where people had to work from eight to six, but "they are paid by the piece, or work they do."

On May 1, 1913, Henry Ford changed the way he made generators for his car. Instead of giving each worker twenty-nine parts to make a generator, he gave twenty-nine workers in a line one part each to add to the growing generator. A little later he powered the line. This invention of the assembly line reduced the time needed to make a generator from twenty minutes to five minutes. Within a year he assembled whole cars this way.

The assembly line was much more efficient, but people could not be paid individually for the work they did because the line moved at a given speed. The workers had to be paid for working a given amount of time rather than for what they produced. Since some people work too hard under piecework conditions, labor unions campaigned for the hourly wage everywhere. Today, nearly everyone is paid for being present an hour rather than for actual work done.

Employers have to pay inexperienced, low-producing adolescents the same as experienced, high-producing older workers. Employers want people who can produce, so adolescents are the last hired and first fired. Adolescents often hear, "Come back when you get some experience."

They say, "How can we get experience if no one will hire us?" They have a good point, but the hourly wage as a basis for pay means that employers will hire them only as a last resort.

Employers also set requirements for jobs, requirements that do not make much sense. For example, many unnecessarily require a high school diploma. A high school diploma today does not even mean that one can read and write. The main thing such a requirement does is to keep anyone under eighteen from getting a job, even if state law says they can work after age sixteen.

What can people do at twenty-one or at eighteen that they cannot do at fourteen or sixteen? Not much, if anything. As we saw in the first chapter, people are adults physically and mentally long before they graduate from high school. Are adolescents inherently less responsible than older persons? No, teenagers were in the work force a century ago. Why keep them from working now?

Although we hear much about age discrimination, it does not usually include adolescents. "Age discrimination" usually means discrimination against people forty to seventy years of age, not those twelve to twenty. Adolescent unemployment has been with us as long as we have had adolescence. Ever since the 1940s when the labor department began keeping unemployment statistics for teenagers, the adolescent unemployment rate has been three to five *times* as large as that of other adults.

Even these statistics do not reveal the extent of the problem. They do not include the adolescents who would be looking for work if they thought they could find it. Three out of four employers do not want to hire people under twenty-one for regular full-time positions. What an introduction to the world of work! Our culture has switched from child labor to young adult unemployment as a way of life.

Legislation has not reduced adolescent unemployment. Congress has created various youth corps and job corps with little lasting effect. The unemployment rate among white sixteen-to-nineteen-year-olds is about the same as in the 1940s, and among blacks it is two or three times as high. Unemployment is a part of adolescence in our culture.

I'll Find Something to Do!

In hearings before the Subcommittee to Investigate Juvenile Delinquency in 1955, Senator Alexander Wiley said, "To me when I see the youth of this country in idleness, walking the streets of the cities, [I feel] we are meeting a challenge to our common sense because we know idleness breeds not only crime but everything else." Not expected to work and not allowed to work, adolescents often find something to do and wind up breaking the law.

Laws have distinguished between children and adults for thousands of years based on the "age of responsibility." Under English common law 800 years ago, children under seven could not commit crimes and those under fourteen could not be punished unless someone could show that they could distinguish right from wrong, intended to do wrong, and understood the consequences of what they did. People over fourteen were treated as adults.

Juvenile delinquency, a part of our creation of adolescence, was officially invented with the passage of the Juvenile Court Act by the Illinois legislature in 1899. In that act a "delinquent child" was defined as "any child under the age of 16 years who violates the law of this State or any City or Village ordinance." Of course, at that time (1899) sixteen was about the age at which boys passed through puberty. This law created separate proceedings for children and adults.

Other states soon followed, and the juvenile justice system was seen as great progress. Juvenile courts were to reform, not punish; to uplift, not degrade; to develop, not crush; and to make worthy citizens, not criminals. On October 5, 1905, when Pennsylvania's Justice Brown ruled its act constitutional, he sounded almost religious when he said it was "for the salvation of children." It was "the way by which the state undertakes to save . . . all children under a certain age, whose salvation may become the duty of the state."

As with other parts of adolescence, as the age of puberty went down, the age of adulthood went up. By 1968 people were treated as children legally until they were eighteen or twenty-one. That year the Uniform Juvenile Court Act was written and approved by the American Bar Association. In it a "child" was a person who was: "(1) under the age of 18 years; or (2) under the age of 21 years who committed an act of delinquency before reaching the age of 18 years."

That is, people would legally remain children for three extra years if they committed a delinquent act before they turned eighteen. A "delinquent act" was one "designated a crime under the law." A "delinquent child" was one "who has committed a delinquent act and is in need of treatment or rehabilitation." These definitions made it clear that people were not expected to take responsibility for their actions until they were eighteen or twenty-one.

Just as teenagers have not been expected to take responsibility for supporting themselves, they have not been held responsible for their criminal acts. Their actions have not been considered crimes. People have seen delinquents as being in need of treatment, not punishment. For thousands of years teenagers were treated legally as responsible adults, but today we treat them as children.

One problem has been that we have made serious crimes rather insignificant. Other adults have long felt that teenagers could "get away with murder." That used to be just an expression, but since the invention of adolescence, it has often become literally true. With the invention of juvenile delinquency, teenagers could commit what would be serious crimes if they were adults, but they would be sent home, not to prison.

In 1980 the National Commission on Youth noted that youth arrests for violent crime (murder, rape, robbery, aggravated assault) were climbing nearly twice as fast as for all crime. The most arrested group in the nation was eighteen-year-olds, second was seventeen-year-olds, then nineteen-year-olds, followed by sixteen-year-olds (*The Transition of Youth to Adulthood: A Bridge Too Long,* National Commission on Youth, Westview Press).

One California delinquent in a training school complained, "I was sent here on a bum rap." The bum rap was not that he was innocent of the robbery, but that "the judge sent me here on the third offense, instead of waiting until the fifth."

As a Minneapolis social worker put it, "If you want to get locked up, run away from home. If you want to be returned home, commit a burglary." She was right. More than four out of five charged with incorrigibility were held, while only about half of those charged with burglary were.

Another problem was just the opposite. We created "crimes" that only adolescents could commit. By about 1960 "delinquency" carried a stigma, so we invented "status offenses" for adolescents "in need of supervision." Instead of delinquents, they became PINS, CHINS, MINS, or JINS (persons, children, minors, or juveniles "in need of supervision").

Adolescents can be taken into custody for doing things other adults can do with no penalty. Other adults cannot commit such crimes as trying to get married or leaving home without permission. About a third of the arrests of adolescents are for crimes that would not be wrong if they were a little older. FBI reports show that 100% of the arrests for curfew, loitering, and runaways are for people under eighteen—since people eighteen and older cannot commit these "crimes." This is another clear case of age discrimination.

The juvenile justice system has been a failure. In 1967, the President's Crime Commission reported that the great hopes originally held for the juvenile court system had not been realized. It had "not succeeded significantly in rehabilitating delinquent youth, in reducing or even stemming the tide of delinquency." The Joint Commission of Juvenile Justice Standards said that a system that "allows the same sanctions for parental defiance as for armed robbery . . . can only be seen as inept and unfair."

Many states now question the idea of not expecting responsible behavior from adolescents. Nine states have no age limit, and most states have laws saying that serious offenders fourteen to sixteen years of age can be tried as adults. Vermont recently lowered its age of accountability to ten. We may be seeing the demise of the juvenile justice system, and that is not all bad. Our laws should make a distinction between children and adults, but not turn adults into children.

What Can Parents Do?
Since the law prevents many teenagers from working and fails to hold them fully responsible for criminal acts, it may seem that

parents can do little to solve these problems. However, parents can do much to help their adolescents learn responsibility.

Find work? Adolescents should learn how to work by having *real* work at home. They need to care for their rooms, help at mealtimes and help with everyday tasks that need to be done around the house. Lawn mowing, painting, and cleaning are adult work, and teenagers should be involved. In our family, parents and teenagers plan and prepare Sunday dinner on alternate weeks. Our three teenagers take turns planning the menu and being in charge of cooking the meal with the others helping. If they forget, we all eat sandwiches.

However, most teenagers are also able to find some kind of part-time work. Our teenagers mow lawns, rake leaves, shovel snow, and baby-sit. Some teens start their own businesses, such as growing vegetables or worms. As parents you should encourage such things. You should also help adolescents avoid some of the commercial ventures, such as envelope stuffing at home, designed to take money from people, not help them earn money.

If possible, help them find work with someone who appreciates what they do. As our teens mowed lawns, it made a real difference whether or not they felt they were doing a service. Some of their customers were grateful, glad to have someone mow the lawn. This made them feel needed, since they were really helping people, not just earning money.

Teens can be a real help and learn much through volunteer work. When our daughter Cheryl was a candy striper at the University of Kentucky Medical Center, she learned about everything from meeting people to helping people to dealing with bureaucratic red tape. She learned how to work with professionals and patients. She was of service, and what she learned was more valuable than many courses she took in school.

Help your teenagers prepare a résumé. They will need it to apply for work and scholarships. If they begin it when they become adolescents and keep it up as they move on through high school, it will be of great value. Our teens learned this through doing record books for 4-H. When it came time to apply to college and for work, all the information was there in usable form.

Teach about work. You need to work with your adolescents as well as assign them work. They learn by example much better than by hearing what they should do. Instead of just sending them out to weed the garden, weed it with them. Paint the house with them. In the past, teenagers learned about work from their parents, and they should still form their attitudes toward work by watching their parents. What you say about your work will profoundly affect how your teens view work. Too often they learn from other adolescents who know little about work themselves.

You need to teach them about things associated with work as well. Teach them to get things done on time. Workers who do not meet deadlines have trouble keeping their jobs. In our culture workers must be able to get out of bed in the morning and make it to their workplaces on time. Parents who take responsibility for getting their teenagers up in the morning and pushing them out the door to catch the school bus are setting them up for problems in the future. Teens can have their own alarms and be responsible for getting up, dressed, and ready for the bus on time.

In a sense, school is an adolescent's work, and their grades evaluate how well they work. Some parents pay their children and adolescents for grades. I don't advocate that because they will soon start learning for the money, and when the money stops, they will stop learning. As one major league baseball player put it, "I used to enjoy playing ball until I started getting paid for it." Adolescents need to be held responsible for their performance in school. Some of their work later will be much like their work in school.

Teach them whatever skills you have. If you know something about car repair, teach it to your adolescents. If you know word processing, teach it to them. The computer on which I am writing this manuscript sits in the family room, and our teens see me working on it daily. All three of our teenagers could type and do word processing before they got to high school simply because it was a part of our life.

Finally, since the state keeps adolescents economically dependent, you have a responsibility to provide for them in the case of your death. In past times other members of your family would probably have taken over responsibility for your dependents. Today the state takes over. You should have a will and a trust set up in which you name a guardian for your adolescents. If you do not, and something happens to you, the state will decide who takes care of them during their crucial teenage years—and the state may not choose the guardian you would choose.

Hold them responsible. Since our juvenile justice laws seem to have things backward, it is up to you to straighten them out as far as your teens are concerned. Take action to prevent your adolescents from becoming involved in criminal behavior and hold them responsible if they do.

To start with, you can see that they do not have too much idle time. If they are not involved in school activities, they should take more responsibility around the house or perhaps work part-time. Wandering the streets too often leads to trouble, and it certainly does not teach responsibility. Confront them when you see them getting involved with the wrong people.

Expect responsible behavior from adolescents, just as you do from other adults. Remember that people act the way you expect them to. If you expect teenagers to act irresponsibly, they will. On the other hand, if you expect them to act as responsible adults, they will. Tell them that as long as they act responsibly, you will treat them as adults. Of course, if they act like children, treat them as such.

Whether or not our society holds our adolescents responsible, God does. Just because our culture does not punish adolescents for breaking its laws does not mean that God will not hold them responsible for breaking His. You must make sure that they understand that He may not hold them responsible for breaking their culture's rules, but He will for breaking His commands. He may not punish them for standing on a corner after ten o'clock, but He will for stealing.

As parents, we may be too protective of our adolescents. As one mother put it, "If I don't stick up for him, who will?" We must hold them responsible for wrong behavior even if the government lets them off. They may get off with a warning for hurting someone or stealing, but we should see that they make restitution for what they have done. Our society has gone too far in "protecting" them when they do something wrong.

We must make distinctions between ignorance of the law, harmless fun, and deliberate criminal acts. If they were not intentionally doing something wrong, we need to stick up for them, but if they knew they were doing wrong, they should be punished. They should also realize that you will hold them responsible for whatever the group they are with does.

When you do something wrong, they should see you apologize and make restitution. You need to be a model, not only in doing right, but in righting wrongs. Help them to realize that they can hurt people psychologically as well as physically and that those hurts need to be corrected too.

As in other areas, we need to treat our adolescents as adults in the area of work and crime. Even if our culture does not hold them responsible, as parents we need to do so.

CHAPTER TEN

A Calling, Some Cash, and Some Credit

As Eric was leaving for a movie with several of his friends, his father handed him a twenty-dollar bill and told him to have fun. He spent it all that evening, knowing there was plenty more where that came from. His father was not wealthy, but since he had grown up without much, he had vowed that his children would have whatever they wanted.

Jenny did not have as much money as Eric, but she could not understand why some people worried so much about it. Her mother seldom worked, but the welfare checks came regularly. It seemed stupid to her for a person to spend time doing a boring job when all you had to do was let the government pay you.

Learning to work is only half of economic independence. The other half is learning to use money. Eric and Jenny are learning neither. As parents you need to teach your adolescents what work means, what they need, and how to manage money.

By the Sweat of Your Brow
At one time work was praised as a right and a duty—a way of serving God. This was the foundation for the Protestant work ethic so prevalent in the United States in the past. However, today many

adolescents make fun of this old ethic which promotes hard work. They do not want to become "workaholics," caught up in their work as some people are in their alcohol.

Even some Christian adolescents have a negative view of work. They read Genesis 3, where work is mentioned along with sin, and they believe that it is a result of breaking God's commandments.

> Cursed is the ground because of you;
>   through painful toil you will eat of it
>   all the days of your life.
> It will produce thorns and thistles for you,
>   and you will eat the plants of the field.
> By the sweat of your brow
>   you will eat your food
> until you return to the ground,
>   since from it you were taken;
> for dust you are
>   and to dust you will return.
>
>   (Gen. 3:17-19)

However, a closer examination of the early chapters of Genesis leads to a positive view of work. "The Lord God took the man and put him in the Garden of Eden to work it and take care of it" (Gen. 2:15). This was *before* sin entered the world. Work was a part of original creation, before sin had affected it.

Not only did Adam and Eve work, but God also worked. "By the seventh day God had finished the work He had been doing; so on the seventh day He rested from all His work. And God blessed the seventh day and made it holy, because on it He rested from all the work of creating that He had done" (Gen. 2:2-3). God certainly would not do something that was a result of sin. Work was a part of God's activity in creating the world. The ability to work is part of the image of God in which we were created.

We were commanded to work in imitation of God. We usually interpret the fourth commandment as demanding rest on the Sabbath. However, it was a command to keep the Sabbath holy, and the elaboration of it began, "Six days you shall labor and do all your work" (Ex. 20:9) just as God did. It was a command to work as well as to rest. People need a balance of work and rest, not just rest.

Part of the problem in our culture is that much of our work is in imitation of the machine, not in imitation of God. God's work was creative, and much modern work is not. Craftspeople of the past could express their God-like creativity as they made things. The assembly-line worker of today does the same thing over and over again, another cog in a giant machine. Rather than concentrating on productivity, we need to concentrate on creating jobs that have a positive effect on the people doing them.

Blind Choices

Too few people have a vocation at the end of their adolescence. Usually they start on their careers, enter occupations, or take jobs. Although these words mean roughly the same thing, they come from different roots. A "vocation" refers to a calling, a call to perform a certain function. "Career" comes from a word meaning road or racecourse. An "occupation" is something that engages (occupies) a person's time and attention. A "job" is something one has to do, a chore or duty.

One of the most common majors among college freshmen is "undecided." With no sense of call, many adolescents ask the wrong questions when choosing their lifework. Their questions usually are "what's -in-it-for-me" questions: questions about salary, fringe benefits, working conditions, hours, vacations, retirement plans, and so on. After they choose their jobs, they find that the benefits are large enough, but the jobs are too small.

Worthy vocations often have low pay. The work is hard, useful, and of public concern. People in important vocations seldom complain about money. When you hear people complaining about the pay, you know that they do not see their jobs as important enough. Since they do not feel useful, they want more money.

Work used to be public, often associated with the home. People knew what nearly everyone else in the community actually did in their work. Today work is separated from the home and is private. It is done at the office, the factory, the shopping center, or the farm away from home. Adolescents may have never actually seen anyone really doing the kind of work they think they want to do. Work is not done in the presence of children and adolescents, so they make blind choices of vocations.

I Need That!

A hundred and fifty years ago most people considered their necessities to be food, clothing, and shelter. A couple could start a marriage on about $100 plus wedding gifts. The man usually received a horse, farm implements, and seed. The woman received a bed, a cow, and kitchen utensils. Relatives put up a house and stable, and in a few years the couple was prospering.

Today so many things are "necessary" for life that people must stay dependent for many years before they can marry. In June 1982, *Good Housekeeping* magazine and the Association of Bridal Consultants published a list of "basic necessities" (their words) needed to set up housekeeping now. The lowest estimate of the cost was $6,025. If you bought better quality items, the cost was $30,479. That did not include food, clothing, house, or car.

Included in the list were two washcloths, two bath towels, two pillows, a table lamp, a frying pan, a saucepan, and a salad bowl. However, also included were crystal (wine and water goblets) for eight at $240 ($1,100 for higher quality), a five-piece china setting for eight at $216 ($2,262 for higher quality), and a five-piece sterling-silver set for eight at $2,592 ($6,640 for higher quality). These were in addition to a five-piece everyday dinnerware set for eight, three-piece glassware service for eight, and stainless-steel flatware for eight.

All of these were listed as "basic necessities" for setting up housekeeping. Our culture has come a long way from food, clothing, and shelter. Food, clothing, and housing were not even included in the list above. A recent newspaper article pointed out that six-to-sixteen-year-olds spend about $45 billion a year on "essentials" (their word), such as "albums, candy bars, comic books, soda pop, and jeans."

Buy Now, Pay Later

Since teenagers cannot work to earn money as they did in the past, they often do not have the chance to learn how to handle it. The best way for them to learn is to actually earn money and spend it for their needs. They never get the chance to learn the value of a dollar, no matter how low it has dropped because of inflation.

Borrowing money has also changed in recent years. At one time people borrowed money to raise capital, money used in trade, manufacture, or business. The purpose of borrowing was to raise capital to make more money. Then the loan would be repaid from the profits. Farmers borrowed money for seed and repaid the loan at harvest time. Merchants borrowed to buy inventory for their stores, then repaid the loan when they sold the goods.

Today however, consumer credit in the form of installment buying is widely used. This borrowing is quite different from raising capital or even borrowing to feed the family until harvest time. Most of this borrowing is simply a matter of not wanting to wait for something. This means that people are paying for the use of money that is not used to make money. Since adolescents cannot get credit cards, they often have trouble using them later.

In eighth grade Jeff started on a two-week trip with the youth group with nearly twice as much money as anyone else. Two-thirds of the way through the trip he was borrowing money from others to eat. As a high school senior he wanted a new stereo but did not have the money. He borrowed $600, hoping that his tax refund would be that much. The last time I saw him he was graduating from college $26,000 in debt and ready to begin working—at the bottom of the salary scale.

Jeff is not unusual. With college costing $5,000–$10,000 a year, it is not at all uncommon for graduates to begin their working lives $25,000–$30,000 in debt. Money is easy to borrow while in college, and adolescents who have never learned to handle borrowing often find themselves deeply in debt.

Pay Now, What Later?

In the preface to his three-volume work, *Children and Youth in America* (Harvard University Press) Robert Bremner, Professor of

History at Ohio State University, said that before 1865 Americans could not support the luxury of a prolonged youth. Young people had to assume the responsibilities of adulthood. We may again be entering a time when we cannot afford this luxury.

It may seem odd to bring up retirement when discussing adolescence, but it may be a major factor in ending adolescence. We invented Social Security and retirement about the same time we did adolescence, and it is unlikely that we can afford both very long. I will talk only about the retirement part of Social Security, although it is a much larger program than that. Required old-age insurance began in Germany in 1889. Similar laws passed in England in 1899, in France in 1928, and in the United States in 1935.

As originally passed, our Social Security system was modeled after good private retirement plans. It was to be financed on a fully funded basis with the taxes invested in trust funds. The money people paid was to be invested for them to use when they retired, and each person's benefits were to depend on the total taxes he or she had paid into the fund.

Unfortunately, changes began almost immediately. In 1939 Congress abandoned the fully funded basis for a pay-as-you-go basis. That is, the taxes paid in were not invested, but given to people who had already retired. Benefits were started early, tax increases were delayed, and benefits were no longer linked to total contributions. This was the beginning of the largest pyramid scheme in history. People thought they were getting something for nothing, but only those who got in early actually did.

Many other changes had to be made to keep the pyramid from collapsing. More and more people were required to pay into it, and each person was required to pay more into it. However, in spite of all that Congress has done, Social Security is still in serious trouble. The problem is that the pyramid has matured. From this point on everyone in it will lose money.

Using a pyramid scheme, we have been able to support people during the first and last eight years of their adult lives. We support people during childhood and adolescence, have them work for forty years, then support them for ten or fifteen years during retirement. We probably cannot continue to afford this. We cannot maintain our standard of living and support people during twenty years of their adult lives. We will probably have to shorten both retirement and adolescence.

What Can Parents Do?

Since the culture makes it difficult for teenagers to learn to manage money, it is up to you, as parents, to teach your own adolescents.

Choosing a vocation. In spite of the connection between work and sin in Genesis 3, work is generally presented in a positive light in the Bible. Like the rest of creation, it has been affected by sin, but it is not sinful. It is an expression of the image of God in each of us. It is basically good.

The Apostle Paul commanded people to work. "He who has been stealing must steal no longer, but must work, doing something useful with his own hands, that he may have something to share with those in need" (Eph. 4:28). In fact, he told the Thessalonians to ostracize those who did not work.

In the name of the Lord Jesus Christ, we command you, brothers, to keep away from every brother who is idle and does not live according to the teaching you received from us. . . . For even when we were with you, we gave you this rule: "If a man will not work, he shall not eat." We hear that some among you are idle. They are not busy; they are busybodies. Such people we command and urge in the Lord Jesus Christ, to settle down and earn the bread they eat. . . . If anyone does not obey our instruction in this letter, take special note of him. Do not associate with him, in order that he may feel ashamed. Yet do not regard him as an enemy, but warn him as a brother. (2 Thes. 3:6, 10-12, 14-15)

Of course, our invention of adolescence with its child labor laws makes it illegal for most teenagers to keep this command. As parents, however, you can see that your teenagers view work as good, as a reflection of God's image in us as human beings. This "theology of work" should be part of what you teach to your children and adolescents about how to choose their vocations. In our culture, you are not likely to choose your adolescents' vocations. However, as in marriage, you must teach your adolescents how to choose. Help them ask the right questions about choosing a vocation. Of course, everyone needs enough money to live, but there are much more important questions to ask. The value of the work itself is more important than the monetary benefits. How many ministers, missionaries, and teachers would we have if financial benefits, hours, and working conditions were the major considerations?

I listened as one teenager described her job of collecting bees to get their venom. She said, "I feel like I'm helping someone, maybe even saving a life. Selling hamburgers just didn't cut it with me." There is nothing wrong with feeding people—Jesus fed them fish—but this young woman was considering the right questions. She was not going to catch bees all her life, but she wanted even her temporary adolescent work to be of value.

This is important not only for the choices they make during adolescence, but also for the choices they will make as they change work in later life. Few people now spend a lifetime in one type of work in our culture. They need to make good choices as they move from one type to another. If your adolescents do not learn how to make good choices now, they will not be able to make good choices later.

Spending money. Your children and adolescents also need to learn to save and spend money wisely. The best way for them to do this is to actually save and spend it. At first they will need much help from you, but by mid adolescence they should be doing it on their own. Parents use several different ways to teach spending and saving.

Howard and Marilyn use an allowance to teach their teens. They give their teens five dollars each week. The teens are responsible for certain things. They must buy all school supplies and all the "extras" they want. They are not responsible for major expenses, like food and clothes, but have to budget their money to meet the minor ones that occur, such as birthday gifts and dates.

Ida and Burt do not like the idea of giving money for no work.

They make their adolescents work for the "allowance." Instead of just having them work around the house as a part of the family, each teen is paid for what he or she does. For example, Bert Jr. gets $10 for mowing the lawn and Lila gets $12 each time she cleans the house.

Rusty and Trixie do not give any money to their adolescents even for work. They tell their teens that they have to work somewhere else for their spending money. The teens then find part-time jobs outside the home to earn their spending money. They mow lawns, baby-sit, and shovel snow.

Finally, Irene and Rodney give their adolescents much larger amounts of money, including money for food at school and for clothing. Each of their teens get fifty dollars a month and it has to be used for lunches on all school days and for all their clothing. Parents and teens agreed on a reasonable amount and the teens get the fifty dollars each month when Rodney is paid. They keep the money in their bank accounts and collect the interest on it. If they spend the money on other things, they just do not get new clothes when the others wear out or are too small.

Whatever method you use, it is important to keep the goal in mind. Remember that you are teaching your adolescents to manage money. You are not only meeting their needs but are also teaching them how to meet those needs themselves when they leave home in a few years.

Another important issue is the use of the family car. This is an added expense when an adolescent starts to drive. Herb's parents made him pay the added insurance costs when he wanted to become a regular driver of the car. This was no small expense since adding a sixteen-year-old male doubled the insurance rates. Helga's parents let her use the car whenever she wanted, but charged her ten cents a mile. Ennis could use the car whenever he wanted, but had to pay for gas used. Whatever arrangement you have, treat your adolescents as adults and expect some pay for the use of the car.

Teenagers should each have their own savings and checking accounts to learn how to manage money in the bank. Adolescents are not too young to be giving to the church regularly. Patterns they begin as children and teenagers will continue through life. They should pledge to the church and contribute regularly, even if it is only a few cents a week or a few dollars a month.

Teach them how to get good value for their money. When thirteen-year-old Adrian wanted a new ten-speed bicycle, his parents pulled out *Consumer Reports* to find which bicycle was best. They thought he should learn not to waste money on cheap products—and not to buy expensive ones if reasonably priced ones were better. Doug and Estelle buy their teens good quality clothing for school, but if the teens want "fad" or "prestige" clothing, they have to pay the extra for it themselves.

Our teenagers know all about our family expenses. Our checkbook and bank statements are not secrets "for parents only." We believe adolescents need to know what it costs to live. They thought $12,000 a year for a starting salary sounded like great wealth until they found out how much heat, lights, insurance, food, house payments (or rent), clothing, and cars cost.

Borrowing money. Since teenagers usually cannot get credit cards from someone else, you may have to teach them about installment buying yourself. Clark wanted a guitar, but did not have the money. His parents agreed to lend him fifty dollars if he would repay it at two dollars a week. He eagerly agreed, but soon found that six months of "easy" payments was no fun. His parents charged no interest, but they demanded payment each week when he got his allowance. He learned a valuable lesson about living in our consumer-credit culture.

As good parents they did not "have mercy" when one of his favorite rock groups came to the local arena in concert. They remembered that they were teaching a lesson. The important thing was that he learn to make payments on time, even when he wanted something else. They insisted on every payment when it was due. Teens must learn not to overextend themselves so that they cannot repay what they borrow. Clark got to hear the concert by borrowing from a friend, but he had to skimp to pay that back.

Sue wanted to borrow from a bank to buy a used car. Her parents agreed that the car was a good one, and she could use it to drive to work. They found this a chance to teach her comparison shopping for loans. Sue quickly became confused by all the different kinds of loans available. Some sounded good, but when Dad pointed out the annual percentage rates, she decided on a simple interest loan. Mom and Dad had to cosign the note, but they made sure it was Sue who made the payments to the bank when they were due.

When Ed and Bev had to borrow money, they made their teenagers a part of it. They let their teens see the steps they took to get it and how they paid it back. When they had to cancel a weekend at the beach because of paying back the loan, they let the teens know why it had to be canceled. They felt it was important for them to see that debts had to be paid.

Simplifying life. Since it is unlikely that our adolescents will have the standard of living we have, we should begin to prepare them for a simpler lifestyle. We can do this by living more simply ourselves. We can use our air conditioning less or not at all. We can grow food in our gardens and have our adolescents help us both grow and preserve it.

We all need to prepare ourselves for a simpler lifestyle. In 1950 there were sixteen workers paying into Social Security for every one drawing benefits. Thus each worker was paying only one-sixteenth of a Social Security benefit. By the time we retire, there will only be three (or possibly two) paying into the system for every one drawing benefits. That means that each worker will have to pay one-third (or one-half) of what each retiree receives. It is unlikely that workers will pay that large a tax.

Realistically, this means that we do need to make some plans for retirement. Newscasters and reporters are beginning to talk about the rise of private pension plans and the demise of Social Security. We need to be aware that the system cannot go on as it is now, but will be changed. We need to take steps to prepare for the future ourselves.

CHAPTER ELEVEN

Do I Have to Go to School?

Karla, a high school freshman, came home from school one afternoon. Bored with school, she said, "Every year we do the same old stuff. We learn about nouns and verbs. We study the history of the United States. I'm bored to death. Do I have to go?"

Jack, also in Karla's class, went home asking the same question, but for different reasons. He said, "I'll never get it. I still can't tell when to use *good* and when to use *well*. They both sound all right to me. What difference does it make what x is? I'll never use algebra anyway. Do I have to go?"

Karla was bored because she learned rapidly and already knew most of what was being taught. Jack learned more slowly, and he felt as though it was just not worth the effort. Since both were teenagers and not allowed to work, our culture had to do something with them. Education seemed like the logical, even practical, thing. Like not allowing them to work, making teenagers go to school was part of our creation of adolescence.

Everyone Must Go

For thousands of years parents educated their own children. They taught whatever was necessary to succeed in society. Our society

143

wants everyone to read and write, to understand the scientific method, to know algebra and geometry, and so on. No country has ever achieved that kind of education by just setting up schools and encouraging parents to send their children. The only way to get it has been to pass laws forcing people to send their children to school.

Modern laws requiring school attendance began in Germany (Prussia) in the seventeenth century. Although the laws existed early that century, they were seldom enforced. More democratic countries did not even pass similar laws until the nineteenth century. People saw those laws as the state taking over what parents should do.

In 1852 Massachusetts passed the first effective law in the United States requiring all children to go to school. According to that law, everyone from eight to fourteen years of age had to go to school twelve weeks a year. It took more than sixty-five years for all the other states to follow. Notice that these early laws did not create adolescence. Children had to attend until they were fourteen, and puberty occurred at fifteen, sixteen, or even later. Children had to go to school, adults did not.

As more laws were passed, legislators lowered the age for starting school, raised the age for quitting, and lengthened the school year. Today Ohio and Utah require everyone from six to eighteen to be in school, a total of twelve years. Mississippi requires only six years, those years from seven to thirteen.

Notice that these laws say that people must spend a given amount of time in school, not that they must learn anything. They are compelled to attend, not to learn. Typical laws state that people must go to school for about 180 days a year for about 6 hours a day for about 10 years. That is, people must spend 10,800 hours in the classroom before they can be fully accepted into the adult world.

Compulsory attendance laws alone did not create adolescence. That first Massachusetts law of 1852 requiring children to attend school until the age of fourteen meant that only children had to go to school. At the same time that the age of puberty decreased to twelve or fourteen, laws were changed to make people attend school until they were sixteen or eighteen. The increase in required schooling at the same time as the decrease in age of puberty was part of our creation of adolescence. With these changes adults (adolescents), not just children, were forced to attend school.

Who Gets Promoted?

Another recent invention and a part of our creation of adolescence is "age grading." This is the practice of putting people in a class (grade) in school, not because of what they know, but because of how old they are. At one time people were promoted to fourth grade because they knew the third grade material, not because they were nine years old.

Age grading began in Germany and was introduced in the United States in 1844. The Quincy Grammar School in Massachusetts was reorganized in 1847 to become the first fully age-graded public school in the United States, and all schools were age graded by 1900. Part of this was motivated by the fear of the "disease of precocity" mentioned in chapter 2. If all the pupils of the same age were in the same grade, none would be considered precocious.

School has become a twelve-year-long assembly line. Once a child starts on it, he or she finds it very difficult to move faster or slower than anyone else. Neither "retention" (failure) nor advancing faster than other people the same age is common. Although bright seventh graders may know more than the average twelfth grader, they are forced to stay on the assembly line for another five years—they keep taking courses, but learning little.

How Long?

Free, compulsory public education at first applied only to the elementary school. High school came later. In fact, the high school is a part of our invention of adolescence.

Most people consider the English Classical School, founded in Boston in 1821, as the first high school. It had a three-year course of study usually completed between twelve and fifteen years of age. This "high school" did not create adolescence because graduates were only fifteen, and the age of puberty was still above that. In 1874 the Michigan Supreme Court ruled that the high school was a proper part of the public school system, and that opened the way for increased development of high schools at public expense. From then on public education increased, and private education declined.

Still, only a few people went to high school until the first half of this century. According to the U.S. Office of Education, in 1890 only 7 out of every 100 people between fourteen and seventeen years old were enrolled in high school. By 1910 it had about doubled to 15 of every 100. It was not until 1930 that even half the people this age were in high school. Today 95 of every 100 are in school. In 1870 only 2% graduated from high school, but in 1970, 75% did.

Support for compulsory education may be on the wane. In 1980 the National Commission on Youth pointed out that school had become a "holding period," serving detention or custodial services. It had become a place of detention, not attention. It kept teens in custody, off the streets during the day, freeing other adults for more efficient production in their work. It also kept them out of the job market so that other adults had the best chances at jobs.

In 1973 the National Commission on the Reform of Secondary Education recommended that the length of required attendance be shortened. Specifically it suggested that it be lowered to fourteen in every state. In 1980 the National Commission on Youth came to the same conclusion. In other words, they were questioning our invention of adolescence. After a century of adolescence, the newest idea is to return to what worked for thousands of years.

College for the masses did not help create adolescence, but it has lengthened it. Most college students are adolescents because they are not economically independent and are not participating fully in adult life. As we require more education by more people, adolescence becomes longer, and problems increase.

Who Is Responsible?

A big question today is, "Who is responsible for education?" Many people believe it is the job of the school system, but that is a new concept, part of our invention of adolescence. Let us look at who was responsible for thousands of years and who should be responsible today.

Parents Did It. Among the ancient Hebrews parents were responsible for the education of their children. The Talmud said, among other things, that the father was to "teach him Torah, take a wife for him, and teach him a craft." Notice that the father had two teaching duties, one religious and one occupational.

Roman parents educated their own children too. Mothers taught both boys and girls reading, writing, and arithmetic. The girls stayed with their mothers, but at about the age of seven boys went with their fathers. If the father was a farmer, the boy went to the fields with him. If he lived in Rome, the boy joined him, learning about business and government.

In the American colonies parents were still responsible for educating their children. In 1774 John Adams wrote his wife about their son, "Tell him I hope to hear a good account of his accidence and nomenclature when I return." He went on to say that the education of his children was never out of his mind.

In Loco Parentis. Although parents were responsible for educating their children, at times they had someone act in their place. Roman fathers too busy to give much attention to their children's education sometimes turned them over to slaves. Although the fathers were still responsible, the slaves were acting in the fathers' places, *in loco parentis,* which means "in the place of a parent."

The word "apprentice" literally means "to learn." The apprenticeship system of the guilds persisted even into the United States. Children were apprenticed for two to ten years to a master workman of good character. The master agreed to teach the boy his trade, to give him food, clothing, and shelter, and to stand *in loco parentis.* The boy agreed to be obedient, not to marry during the training, to keep the secrets of the craft, and to work faithfully.

Problems arose when some parents and masters in the Massachusetts Bay Colony did not fulfill their obligations. The colony passed a law that the selectmen of each town were to watch the "calling and employment of children," and "especially of their ability to read and understand the principles of religion and the capital laws of the country." If they found children not getting such an education they were to apprentice the children to masters who would teach them. This was a new day in education. The state began to act in the place of parents.

Under the concept of *in loco parentis* teachers and administrators began to play the role of the parent when the child was in school. This was not only in regard to the content of their schoolwork, but also in regard to behavior. They regulated hair length, clothing styles, and social practices. This took place not only at the elementary level, but in grammar school, the academy, and the college.

The State Does It. It was only one more step to move from the state acting in the place of the parent to the state taking the place of the parent. Today most educators see themselves as having primary responsibility, with the parents' role being to cooperate with them. For example the "Code of Conduct For the Jessamine County Schools" which our teens brought home this year says that all parents are expected to "cooperate with, show respect to, and lend support to the teachers, administrators and other school personnel."

What Can Parents Do?

Parents are ultimately responsible for all of their children's education, and formal education is important in our culture. Finding work often depends on carrying the "union card" of a high school diploma or a college degree. Dropouts are simply considered last when it comes to getting most jobs. Advancing in many organizations depends more on what formal degrees one has than on what the person contributes.

There is nothing wrong with being in school 1,800 minutes a week. The problem comes when your adolescents are just putting in their time, rather than learning. The state requires only that they be physically present. You need to emphasize that they must learn too. Ask them what they are learning and let them know that it is important to you. Also be sure they realize that their future depends, to some extent, on what they learn, not just on how much time they put in.

Regardless of your teenagers' abilities, you should advise them.

High school counselors are good sources of advice, but the final responsibility is yours. You know their abilities, their motivation, and their attitudes toward school better than anyone else. You are in the best position to advise them. Curriculums are generally geared for average students, so let us consider what to do for those who are below or above average.

For slow learners. If your children or teenagers learn more slowly than average, find a program from which they can profit. If they are having difficulty, help your teens at home and get them into courses where they can succeed. Do not deny the problem, solve it. Gail's parents could not admit that she was below average. The school counselor put her into prealgebra in ninth grade, but her parents insisted on algebra. Gail spent a frustrating year and got a D. Her parents' pride actually hurt her progress.

In contrast, Seth's parents met with the teacher to find out what the problems were. They helped Seth set up a study schedule and then helped him stick to it. They realized that if he missed only two or three important concepts in some courses, it might mean that he would never be able to catch up. Three times when they could not help him they found a tutor who could explain it to him. Seth had a good freshman year and looked forward to his sophomore year.

Encourage them in areas where they succeed. If they have trouble with math and science but are good in art, music, or athletics, encourage them there. Help them to see that their worth does not depend only on what they do in certain courses. Let them see that you love, accept, and value them for what they are, even if they do not get high grades in all courses.

Be patient with them. Even if they are trying, they may take much longer, and even then they may not be able to accomplish what others do. Work with them during summers and evenings to help them as much as possible. Taking that time may mean you will not be promoted in your own career as fast as you had hoped, but it is well worth it.

If you believe your teens' best abilities are in vocational education, encourage them into it. When they realized that Bill would never even be admitted to college, much less graduate from it, his parents enrolled him in a job training program. Today he is happy, self-supporting, and productive. If they had insisted on his trying to make it in college, he probably would have been frustrated the rest of his life.

For fast learners. If your children are fast learners, you face very different problems. Rather than being frustrated, they may be bored. Supplement what they get at school with extra reading and projects at home. These teens can channel their extra time and talent into other areas, such as art, music, reading, or athletics.

Many schools today have special programs for gifted children. Monica was far above average, so her parents put her in the program for gifted teens. She was able to learn much on her own, far more than she would have in a normal classroom. Her parents encouraged her to learn with understanding, not just learn what was necessary to pass.

Meet with their teachers and suggest that your teens be given more challenging problems than average students. Since Kevin did so well in math, they talked with his teacher, suggesting that Kevin tutor slower students in the class. The tutoring helped not only the slower students, but Kevin himself as he found he had to understand geometry better to teach it. Teachers can often use superior students as teacher's aides to make up problems or grade tests.

Many special programs exist for such students. Our own state has a "Governor's Scholars" program in which 600 top students attend special programs on university campuses for part of the summer to study—at no charge. Some summer camps teach computer science, music, and other subjects. Colleges often offer courses to students between their junior and senior years of high school and apply the credit to the students' records when they come to college.

Be careful not to overemphasize academics to the point that your teen's social development is hurt. Some such teens become proud and are rejected by others in school. You want to rear an all-around person, not an adolescent who can do nothing but academics. Encourage them to become involved in athletics, band, and other extracurricular activities.

If your teens need college to prepare for their vocations, they need your help as much as possible. Parents have always been responsible for preparing their children to participate in society, and today that often includes college. We have told our teens that we will do all we can to see that they get a college education. That is a promise based on the condition that they do their best in classes. If they do not study, we will not pay.

Alternatives. Some parents cannot find suitable programs in the public schools of their communities, but that does not mean all is lost. Today good private schools exist in many communities. Sheldon and Maxine sent their teens to a Christian high school in which subjects were taught from a Christian perspective. Since it was not accredited, they investigated it thoroughly to see that it would provide a good education. Many parents today find this a good alternative to the education the state provides.

In some instances parents teach their children at home. Jason and Clara took their teens out of high school and put them in an Accelerated Christian Education program. Both of their children moved rapidly through their grades and on to the next. The parents were delighted, but the teens felt left out socially. They had no teams and no clubs. They finally increased their activity in the church youth group to have more social life.

Remember that whether you teach your teens at home or not, you are their model. If they see you reading and learning, they will develop life-long patterns of learning. If your intellectual diet consists of the front page, the comics, and the sports section of the newspaper, your teens will choose the same.

College credit can also be earned through alternative means. Our son tested out of a year of college through CLEP (College Level Examination Program) and AP (Advanced Placement) tests. Some colleges give credit for work experience. Others offer credit for correspondence work. Scholarship help is available on the basis of both merit and need.

The primary responsibility for educating your teenagers is yours. If you do not educate them, the state will step in and do it. You can determine the kind of formal education your teens get, or you can leave it up to the state.

As parents, you are also responsible for education that takes place outside the schools. This includes religious education as well as teaching teens social and practical skills.

Religious education. Moses specified that the parents had responsibility for the religious education of their children. This was not the responsibility of the priests, but of the parents at home. "These commandments that I give you today are to be upon your hearts. Impress them on your children. Talk about them when you sit at home and when you walk along the road, when you lie down and when you get up. Tie them as symbols on your hands and bind them on your foreheads. Write them on the doorframes of your houses and on your gates" (Deut. 6:6-9).

Moses not only told them *when,* but *how* to go about the religious education of their children. When our children ask us why they have to keep God's commandments, we are not to say, "Because God says so," but to review our identity as God's children. Then we are to make it plain that God has given us these commandments to give us the best lives possible. "The Lord commanded us to obey all these decrees and to fear the Lord our God, so that we might always prosper and be kept alive, as is the case today" (Deut. 6:24). Too often we present God's commands as something to spoil our fun. God gave them to us as the best means of living full lives.

Of course, the Christian Education Department of your church can be a great help in the religious education of your children and adolescents, but the final responsibility is yours. You should be involved in the Sunday School program of your church, helping educate other people's children and adolescents as well as your own.

Social skills. When they begin to think like adults, adolescents are exercising a new ability in critical thinking and forming arguments. Their thinking may not be completely logical, so you need to help them with it just as you helped them learn to walk or ride bicycles. Too often parents who encourage walking when their children are a year old try to discourage thinking when their children become teenagers. These parents take offense at the criticisms made by their teenagers.

Instead of knocking down their arguments, you need to help them think more clearly—and admit it when you fall short yourself.

The best way to argue is to keep arguments about nonemotional matters. Rather than discussing personalities, discuss issues. Turn the discussion to actions the adolescents can take, and place responsibility on them. When Clyde was critical of the government for not conquering world hunger, his parents asked what he was doing about it himself. Then they complimented him on his thinking and joined him in giving to a relief organization. You can do the same whether the criticism is of church, school, or family.

Your children and teenagers will learn about being husbands, wives, mothers, and fathers from you. In addition, you need to teach them how to get along with people in general. Of course, much of this takes place right in your own home. Your children and adolescents learn to relate to authority the way they relate to you. You should be a model in terms of how you relate to those in authority over you, and how you relate to others under your authority. They learn how to get along with people their own age by getting along with brothers and sisters.

Nicole and Grace were not on speaking terms. They communicated with each other through Nelson, their brother. Mom let it go on for a couple days, hoping they would work it out themselves. Finally, she called them together and said, "Nelson, I know you want to help, but what you are doing isn't helping. Nicole and Grace, we won't try to place the blame for this on either of you, but I want you two to start talking to each other. People have to talk to get their differences worked out."

Some of it takes place between "friends." Leland came home with a bruise on his cheek and torn pants. He was talking with his dad about how he would get back at Jerome by letting the air out of his tires that night. Dad listened for a while, then gave some advice about how to handle conflict. He talked about soft answers turning away wrath, and suggested some better ways to handle anger.

Practical skills. Your teens need to learn to do many everyday things that you do without thinking. They will be delighted to learn some, but not want anything to do with others. Both men and women need to learn these. Times change, so these may well be different from what you learned as a teenager.

153

They need to learn how to get around in the world. A century ago this meant learning to ride a horse or drive a team. Today it means learning to drive the car. Most teens are eager to learn this part of living. For some it is an exciting "rite of passage" to get a driver's license. Others may be reluctant, but all need to learn.

Part of learning how to get around is knowing how to maintain your transportation. Today few people need to know how to curry or feed a horse, but they do need to know how to wash a car, check the oil, and pump gas at a self-service pump. They may not be as excited about this part as actually getting behind the wheel, but it is necessary.

They need to know how to maintain a home. A century ago they needed to know how to chink the logs and split wood. Today they need to know how to use a caulking gun and change the furnace filters. They should know how to run a lawn mower and use a paint brush.

Both men and women need to know the basics of cooking and cleaning. Rather than needing to know how to build a fire in the kitchen stove, they need to know how to program the microwave. Scrub boards are not used much any more, but college students visit the laundromat frequently, and they need to know how to sort clothes and what temperatures to use for the different loads. They should learn this at home.

Of course, this list will be different for every family, depending on where they live. People who live in high-rise apartments may not learn about gardening and lawn mowing. Those who live on a farm may not learn about subway schedules and how to get transfers on buses.

This chapter could go on and on. Nearly everything you do can help your adolescents learn, and you learn along with them. Although schools continue to expand the subjects they offer, there will always be things your teens will best learn from you.

CHAPTER TWELVE

You Can Do It!

Carl listened as Jean ended a phone conversation with her mother.

"Yes, Mother. We'll be careful," said Jean. There was a moment of silence as Mom talked at the other end of the line.

"We have plenty of ice. We'll see you after the weekend. Goodbye," finished Jean.

Carl knew what was coming. As she hung up the phone, Jean said, "I'm forty-six years old. I know enough to keep the potato salad cold. We always stop at every second or third rest area so that we don't get too tired. Why does she keep treating me like a child?"

Before Carl could reply, eighteen-year-old Mark came in. "I'll see you two after while. Bob and I are going to get a pizza before we turn in."

"All right," said Jean. "Be sure you have enough money to pay for it. Don't stay too long because you have a test in biology tomorrow, and be quiet when you come in because we are going to bed now."

As soon as Mark was out of hearing, Carl said, "Think about what you just said, Jean. You're treating Mark the way your mother treats you. He knows to take money when he goes to buy something. He knows that he has a test tomorrow, and he's always quiet when he comes in. You're treating him like a child too."

"But he's only eighteen," said Jean. "He has so much to learn. I've been gone from home for twenty-five years and have nearly raised a family. Mom shouldn't still be treating me like a child."

Carl said, "Jean, he's eighteen and legally an adult. The state treats him like the adult he is. You can do it too. It's hard for me to think of him as an adult, but he really is. If you're not going to do it now when he's eighteen, when are you going to do it?"

Like Jean, you may find it very difficult to treat your adolescents as the adults they are. In early adolescence nearly everyone treats teenagers as children, so it is "natural" for you to treat yours that way too. In late adolescence the law begins treating them as adults, but many parents keep treating them as children.

During my junior year in college, as I was about to leave to drive six hundred miles home during Christmas break, my mother wrote, "Keep a flashlight with fresh batteries in your glove compartment. Be sure to keep your gas tank full so you don't run out of gas."

I took the letter home and assured her that I always kept a good flashlight in the car, and whenever the fuel gauge went below half full, I filled the tank. It was hard for her to think of me as an adult.

For the last twenty-five years that has been part of our family good-bye, as a reminder that the "kids" are now adults. Mom and Dad are retired now, and as they left our home last week to drive to my sister's, I said, "Be sure to keep your gas tank full, and keep a flashlight in the glove compartment."

A Final Exam!

At the end of a book written by a college professor you would expect to find a final exam. Here it is. This final exam is different from most finals in that the "right" answer is always obvious. You can get a perfect score and look like a perfect parent if you wish, but that will not do you any good. As you take the test, be honest about what you would do in each situation.

Also, rather than marking in the book, write your answers on a separate sheet of paper. Then ask your teenager or teenagers to take the test as well, answering each question as they think you would respond in that situation. You can then compare how you view yourself with how your teens view you.

Finally, this is not a test of what you know, but a test of what you do (or would do) when the situations come up. Each chapter ended with a section titled "What Can Parents Do?" This test is about what you *do* in real life, not about what you know you *should do.* I have simply taken two situations from each chapter, beginning with chapter two, Give yourself one, two, three, four, or five points for each of the following, according to this scale: 5 = definitely yes; 4 = probably yes; 3 = perhaps; 2 = doubtful; 1 = no.

1. Your teenage daughter does not like peas. She has broccoli and salad on her plate. Do you let her skip eating the peas?

2. You have just finished watching a special on television with your teens. A morally questionable program comes on. Do you give your teenagers a chance to object to the nature of the program before you turn it off?

3. Your family is invited to a potluck supper next door where a group of neighbors is getting together. Do you go and spend time with your neighbors to make your area a real "neighborhood" (whether you live in a city or on a farm)?

4. Your teens want to have a "Christian contemporary music" party at your house with a group of their friends from the church. Do you encourage them to have the party even though you like gospel music better?

5. Your teenagers want the family to camp at the same park where you have vacationed for the last five years. You have enough money this year to stay in a condominium. Do you keep the family tradition that is special to your teenagers?

6. This year the family reunion is over a hundred miles away. Do you take your family even though it comes at the end of a very busy week and you feel more like relaxing at home?

7. It is time for family devotions. Do your teenagers participate equally with other adults in the family?

8. As your family is getting into the car after church, one of the Sunday School children asks your teenagers about the "moonies."

Do you remain silent and let your teens explain?

9. You discover that your teenagers have some soft-core pornography. Do you confront them with the dangers of it?

10. When you are talking with your teenagers about sexual temptations, they say that you do not understand. Do you share some of your own struggles with them?

11. Your teenager's date goes further than is proper in expressing affection. Do you talk again with your teen about what is appropriate in expressing affection physically?

12. Your adolescent asks you about the Bible's position on premarital sex. Can you present it?

13. Your teenagers are dating "nice" Christians, but you want them to date someone from a "better" background. Do you let them keep dating the same persons?

14. Your adolescents say that love is all that matters in marriage. Can you adequately discuss with your teenagers what it takes to make a marriage work?

15. Your teenager has just finished mowing and trimming the neighbor's lawn. Do you stay at home rather than go and check what he or she did?

16. Your teenagers and some of their friends were involved in some vandalism, and all the other parents have paid for the damage their teens did. Do you make your teens pay for their part themselves?

17. Your teenagers are beginning to choose their vocations. Do you basically sit back and watch, confident that you have given them a good basis for choosing?

18. Your teenager wants to borrow money for something you approve. The bank insists on a cosigner. Do you sign the note?

19. A disagreement erupts between your teen and a man down the block. Can you hold your tongue, confident that your teenager can argue effectively and tactfully for his or her own position?

20. Your teenager has a test tomorrow, but she has only studied about a half-hour at home. Her grades are suitable, and now she wants to go to a ball game. Do you let her go?

Do you Pass?

Total your score and see how close you come to getting 100. The higher your score, the more you are treating your adolescents like adults. The lower your score, the more you are treating them like children.

Students in my classes usually want to know what grade they would get on every test. If I were grading the test for someone who had a junior or senior in high school, I would use the following scale.

A = 95–100
B = 85–94
C = 70–84
D = 60–69
F = 0–59

To get an A you would have to treat your teenagers as responsible adults three-fourths of the time and be likely to treat them like that the rest of the time. If you are doing less than that by the time they are in the last couple years of high school, you have room for improvement.

If your adolescents are in the last years of college, I would certainly raise the standard for an A. They have been away from home for a couple years and you definitely need to regard them as the adults they are.

If your teens are in junior high school, I would lower the scale for an A. Our culture expects so little of early teens that you may have real difficulty expecting what they are actually capable of at this time in their lives. This does not mean that you should not expect the best of them, but that you are really fighting our culture to do so.

If Not Now, When?

You may say, "Our adolescent is only fourteen or fifteen. That's too young to expect him or her to behave as a responsible adult. You can't expect people that young to know how much they need to study for the test they have coming up tomorrow."

If you do not expect it of them now, when will you? When they leave home and go to college, will they suddenly know how much they need to study? I believe it is better for them to get a low grade in junior high, where transcripts are not even sent to colleges and are largely forgotten in the future, than to have it on a college transcript that will follow them throughout life.

I have seen too many college students who do not know how to get out of bed in time to get to class. They do not know how to study. They are not disciplined enough to study for tests. I always think, *If only their parents had helped them develop some self-discipline while they were still at home.* Such students tell me how much their parents did for them, and I tell them they would be better off if their parents had done less.

If you do not expect responsible behavior of them now, when will you? Will you when they marry? Does going through the marriage ceremony suddenly give them the ability to handle money? Money is one of the most common causes of friction—and divorce—in marriage. If you do not expect responsible management of money now, you will be making their adjustment to marriage in the future more difficult.

Will getting a job suddenly teach them how to work? A friend of mine working in industry as a chemist says, "The technical problems are simple compared to the interpersonal problems on the job." He has found that getting people to work together is far more difficult than solving chemical problems.

Teenagers who have not learned to work from their parents have to get on-the-job training. This often results in losing several jobs in the process of learning how to work. That may lead to a poor work record and trouble getting the positions they really want.

There is no better time and place to become an adult than during the teen years while a person is at home. Of course, teens make mistakes, but it is much better to make these errors at home in the presence of understanding parents than to make them elsewhere where they will be more costly.

You may say, "I realize I should let my teens act as responsible adults, but I just can't let them go!" Some parents have a real problem letting their children grow up to act as adults. This is often a problem with the parents themselves. You may not be aware of it, but the problem may not be immaturity on the part of your reens, but a reluctance on your part to let them grow up.

There are many reasons for not wanting your teens to become adults, but we will discuss only a few here. Adam would not let his teenagers act like the adults they were because he believed that if they were adults, it meant he was getting old. He would no longer be considered one of the "young adults" at the church.

Before he could let his teenagers be adults, he would have to realize what his problem was. Finally, he accepted it when some of his friends lovingly talked with him about it. He realized that the empty-nest years were usually the years of greatest satisfaction, not of emptiness.

Edna would not let her teens be adults because she would not give up her "helper" role. She had been a helper to her children for nearly twenty years because her four children were born years apart. When the youngest one was in sixth grade, she was still helping dress him for school in the morning. She was afraid to let him grow up because she would have no one to help.

Finally, her husband was able to convince her to let her own children grow up. He did this by getting her involved in helping less fortunate, younger children in the community. She became involved in both Brownies and Cub Scouts where she was a real helper to children, rather than a hindrance to allowing teenagers grow up.

Larry had been a very successful young businessman, achieving his major career goal by age thirty-five. In doing so, he had neglected spending time with his children in their younger years. As they were becoming teenagers, he took the time to attend family life seminars and read books on parenting. When he realized that he had been a poor father, he felt very guilty.

Just as his teens wanted to become adults, Larry was trying to treat them as children to relieve his own guilt. He was trying to be a good father now, but it was too late for the kinds of things he was doing. It was only when his pastor helped him deal with his guilt feelings that he was able to let his teenagers act like the adults they were.

Some parents have thoroughly enjoyed their children. As those children become teenagers, it means that they will be leaving home—if not physically right away, at least they will begin leaving emotionally. Bruno and Phyllis would have passed this chapter's final exam with flying colors when Laura was fourteen, but treating her as an adult was still difficult for them. They did it not because it was easy and felt natural, but because they were convinced it was best for Laura.

Do It Now!

Our culture has created adolescence and handed it to you. Perhaps sometime in the future adolescence will again disappear, but you and your teenagers have to live with it today. As in the past, someday in the future teenagers may be treated as the adults they are, rather than as children, but for now you must struggle with it. Our culture leaves you little choice.

After reading this book you are in a better position to cope with the problems adolescence creates. Now you understand yourself and your teenagers better. Now you are at least asking the right questions. You have a better chance of developing adequate answers. The key, as we have seen over and over, is to recognize that adolescents are adults who are treated like children. The solution is to treat them like the adults they are.

Now that you understand, it is your responsibility to pass this understanding on to your own teenagers. Most of them do not realize why they wonder who they are, struggle with their sexuality, hate school, and wish they had more money. You are responsible to teach them about themselves. Self-understanding itself can help them. If they can understand themselves, and if you treat them as adults, you and your teenagers have made a great start toward solving the problems handed to you.

Of course, if you have been treating them like children, you cannot just suddenly tell them they are adults and they should act like it. They need your help in gradually assuming responsibility. It is important that you start immediately. To get some idea of where to start, look at the final exam you took at the beginning of this chapter. Remember that the test included two questions from each chapter, beginning with chapter 2. Find the areas in which you were falling the shortest and begin there. For example, questions three and four were from chapter 3. If you had low scores on these questions, look over chapter 3 and begin there.

Although I called it a final exam, it is really a progress report. It is "final" in the sense that it comes at the end of this book. However, you should take it every three months or so to see if you are making progress toward treating your teens as adults. Have your teenagers repeat it too. Then have them replace some of the questions with questions of their own so that you find out in what areas they feel you are treating them like children. That will give you some new areas to work on. That kind of individualized test is much more valuable than the general one in this chapter. Then repeat the test (using their new questions) three months later.

Of course, you may do everything "right" as parents, and your teens still not become the kind of persons you want them to be. Remember that they are adults and can make choices on their own. Some of those choices will be wrong ones. The suggestions in this book only help steer them in the right direction, not ensure that they make the right choices. As we saw at the end of chapter 1, understanding adolescence makes the task of being a parent easier, not simple. Ultimately you must commit your teens to God and pray for them constantly.